IMAGES
of America

FREEPORT THROUGH THE YEARS

Named for Christopher Strout, a Falmouth wharf owner who purchased the land from Thomas Maines in 1760, Strouts Point has been an area of prolific commercial activity for more than two centuries. Alexander Motley built a wharf and store here around 1802, and development continued with Strouts Point Wharf Company in 1831, which leased to fishermen and shipbuilders. Men are shown constructing a wharf pump house for fire protection during the World War I shipbuilding period. (Courtesy of Freeport Historical Society.)

On the Cover: This c. 1890 photograph shows workers using a galamander, four yoke of oxen, and a team of horses to haul a large granite stone from entrepreneur Edmund B. Mallet Jr.'s 35-acre quarry on Torrey Hill. Stopped at the railroad crossing on Bow Street, they are headed either to the monument shop for stone dressing or to the freight house for shipping. (Courtesy of Freeport Historical Society.)

IMAGES
of America

FREEPORT THROUGH THE YEARS

Holly K. Hurd
with the Freeport Historical Society

ARCADIA
PUBLISHING

ISBN 978-1-4671-2734-9

Published by Arcadia Publishing
Charleston, South Carolina

Printed in the United States of America

Library of Congress Control Number: 2017937874

For all general information, please contact Arcadia Publishing:
Telephone 843-853-2070
Fax 843-853-0044
E-mail sales@arcadiapublishing.com
For customer service and orders:
Toll-Free 1-888-313-2665

Visit us on the Internet at www.arcadiapublishing.com

This book is dedicated to Eleanor Houston and Lawrence M.C. Smith, who founded their visions of the future on preservation of the past—in gratitude for Pettengill Farm and Harrington House. (Photograph by Kathryn Schneider Smith.)

Contents

ACKNOWLEDGMENTS

The Freeport Historical Society supported production of this work and, unless otherwise noted, provided the historical photographs. In addition, the society's archives, maintained since 1977, were the primary source of research and reference material for interpreting the images. Freeport Historical Society thereby played a central role in this publication by exercising its mission to collect, preserve, develop, and share historical artifacts and documents that tell the stories of Freeport's past.

For its entire near 50-year existence, the staff, volunteers, trustees, society members, monetary and collections donors, program presenters and attendees, and other behind-the-scenes advocates have been the heart and soul of the society. Importantly, the foundations of the society have been maintained by major gifts from Eleanor H. and L.M.C. Smith, and more recently from Joyce and George Denney. Those who care about the past, both today and over the society's lifespan, are acknowledged as vital for the realization of a project such as this book. Research on the photographs benefited from the prior work and knowledge of others, in particular Sally Rand, Mary Eliza Wengren, Vicki Lowe, Randall Wade Thomas, Patricia Anderson, John Mann, Sherry Dietrich, and David Coffin. Thanks are given to them and also to those who generously donated photographs from their collections.

INTRODUCTION

A handful of settlers living in the area that is now Freeport were driven out twice by wars with the Native Americans in the 17th century. According to a map by mariner Cyprian Southack, the first permanent settlements were on Wolfe's Neck, Flying Point, Staples Point, and near the mouth of the Cousins River in the 1720s. Freeport was once part of the larger North Yarmouth, established in 1680, a name that reflects its location relative to Yarmouth in Massachusetts, of which Maine was a part until 1820. The coastal settlements were still tenuous and were threatened until cessation of the French and Indian War around 1760. After that, English settlers from Massachusetts began moving to "Harraseeket"—Freeport's early name, which was also the name of its river—for the area's timber, fish, fertile marshlands, deepwater ports, and mill sites. Some ventured inland where removal of valuable trees was opening the land for farmsteads. By 1774, Harraseeket had enough residents to build its own Congregational church, and in 1789, Freeport was set off from North Yarmouth as an independent town. By 1805, Baptist and Universalist congregations had also been established.

Like many other ministers throughout New England, Rev. Reuben Nason developed a historical interest in the town he served in the early 19th century. Observing and expounding on a town's people, homes, schools, industry, institutions, and roads, with an eye toward leaving a historical record, seems to have been a natural consequence of tending the flock. Installed as Freeport's third Congregational minister in 1810, at the end of Nason's pastorate five years later, he wrote the most comprehensive historical sketch we have of that early period. According to Nason, in 1816, the town had two or three sawmills (Mast Landing, North Freeport), three or four gristmills (Mast Landing, North Freeport, a tide mill on Wolfe's Neck), and two carding machines (Mast Landing). Lumbering, fishing, and shipbuilding were the primary industries at the time, and because Freeport was a port town, transportation networks and trade were also important to the economy. The town had three taverns on the stagecoach route (Means-Holbrook, Jameson, and one on Pleasant Hill Road), and 10 retail stores to service townspeople and those passing through. The minister bemoaned the clay soils that made roads impassable for much of the year, and the very few apple trees and no "cyder mills" in the early 19th century.

Reverend Nason noted there were 11 one-room schoolhouses in the many districts throughout the town, and these were maintained by district taxes. When Maine became a state in 1820, state taxes helped support district schools, and in the 1870s, the town began centrally managing school budgets to account for differences in wealth between districts. The first Congregational minister, Rev. Alfred Johnson, was also the town's first schoolteacher, as was common in 18th-century Maine towns. The original district schoolhouses, built in the decades after Freeport became a town in 1789, had fireplaces. Stoves were added when the schools were rebuilt, generally 50 to 75 years later. Students met no more than 20 weeks a year in the late 19th century, and less than that in the generations before. Some teachers lived in town; those hired from other areas boarded with local families. In the 19th century, teachers were generally single women, although men were also employed, particularly in the districts where students were unruly. In addition to teaching, they did all the cleaning, carried water and wood, and kept the warming fires burning.

According to Reverend Nason, the first settlements were in the western part of town, the area around Cousins River, and the middle and eastern sections, including Porter's Landing and Mast Landing, which were settled in the 1760s. (Apparently, he was unaware of the settlers at Wolfe's Neck and Flying Point.) Although little is known about early settlements on "the Neck" (Lambert and Foggs Points), a tide mill built on Redding's Creek around 1750 may have supplied inhabitants with gristmill and sawmill power. Promontories and waterways were the sites of earliest occupation since travel was primarily by water before roads were laid. The villages of Mast Landing and Porter's Landing, and later South Freeport, grew up as waterside areas of commerce.

Mast Landing was the site of Freeport's first major commercial activity, which was harvesting trees, the so-called "king's broad arrow pines," for the Royal Navy. By the early 1800s, a village had grown up there with a school, stores, blacksmiths, a shoemaker, shipyard, and brickyards as well as a number of residential homes. Schooners and at least one brig were built and launched from the landing. Bricks, salt hay, sawn lumber, and cordwood were shipped out from the wharves to other parts of Freeport and beyond. Some products were carried by the steamer *Tyro*, which had a hinged smokestack allowing it to pass under the bridge to the mill site upstream. The steamer *Harraseeket* once carried passengers between Mast Landing and Portland for a fare of 50¢.

Mast Landing and Porter's Landing developed mutually beneficial commercial ties attributable to their complementary resources and differing geographies. Goods for Mast Landing stores came from shipments to Porter's Landing, and the latter received milled products for shipbuilding from the former. With a deepwater port that supported trade, a saltworks, tanyards, and ice-cutting facilities, Porter's Landing became a thriving village centered around the shipbuilding industry from the late 18th century through 1870. South Freeport had a shipping wharf by the early decades of the 19th century, and from the mid- to late 19th century, it grew into a prosperous village with the coming of the Soule, Bliss, and Talbot shipyards. Every village in Freeport had one or more blacksmiths, stores, schools, shoe shops, and village-specific industries.

Development of the inland Freeport Village was dependent on the coming of roads, which were built and maintained by those who lived in the areas the roads served. Where roads were laid determined where villages grew up, typically at crossroads. Like Mast Landing and Porter's Landing, by the early 19th century, Freeport Village had become an active commercial center where the c. 1770 road from Porter's Landing to Durham crossed the County Road from Portland to Brunswick.

The King's Highway was the first system of roads that ran along the coast or riverways of Maine connecting colonial settlements. It extended from Kittery to Portland in 1653 and had made its way to "Kennebeck" (Hallowell) by 1687, thus claiming distinction as the first road through Freeport. No known records describe the location of this 17th-century road, although it probably followed the coast, past the homesteads of early settlers, as it did farther south. This highway was a simple marked path through the woods, passable only on foot or horse. In 1739, the first County Road was cleared between Portland and Brunswick. Like the earlier pathway through Freeport, it was similarly crude, probably only able to be traveled on horseback or in a heavy-wheeled oxcart. This road largely followed modern-day Route 1, although it meandered to accommodate local topography. Bridges were built over both branches of the Cousins River in 1742, which made travel between current Yarmouth and Brunswick possible by land.

In 1761, the earlier County Road was improved, trees and roots were cut back, and surfaces were graded with dirt and gravel to facilitate travel and mail distribution and foster colonial growth after the French and Indian War. Named the Post Road, this modern roadway was envisioned by Postmaster General Benjamin Franklin and had granite markers placed at mile intervals to indicate distance from Boston. (Six of these markers set in 1761 are still present in Cumberland County today; however, none have survived in Freeport.) Although much improved, the Post Road was still crude, particularly in remote areas. In 1765, future president John Adams traveled over this road on his way from Boston to the Lincoln County Courthouse and wrote that it was

Contents

Acknowledgments

The Freeport Historical Society supported production of this work and, unless otherwise noted, provided the historical photographs. In addition, the society's archives, maintained since 1977, were the primary source of research and reference material for interpreting the images. Freeport Historical Society thereby played a central role in this publication by exercising its mission to collect, preserve, develop, and share historical artifacts and documents that tell the stories of Freeport's past.

For its entire near 50-year existence, the staff, volunteers, trustees, society members, monetary and collections donors, program presenters and attendees, and other behind-the-scenes advocates have been the heart and soul of the society. Importantly, the foundations of the society have been maintained by major gifts from Eleanor H. and L.M.C. Smith, and more recently from Joyce and George Denney. Those who care about the past, both today and over the society's lifespan, are acknowledged as vital for the realization of a project such as this book. Research on the photographs benefited from the prior work and knowledge of others, in particular Sally Rand, Mary Eliza Wengren, Vicki Lowe, Randall Wade Thomas, Patricia Anderson, John Mann, Sherry Dietrich, and David Coffin. Thanks are given to them and also to those who generously donated photographs from their collections.

"greatly incumbered [*sic*] by stumps and roots of interlocking trees . . . wet and miry . . . [and] with great difficulty passable and . . . very hazardous." In spite of these challenges, the Post Road became the main artery of travel through Freeport in the 18th century, and other town roads fed into it from individual farmsteads or village areas. In 1771–1772, British cartographer Joseph Frederick Wallet DesBarres oversaw a survey that mapped the roads in Freeport at the time, which were the Post Road and roads to Durham, the Neck (near Cousins River), Weston Point (later Cushing-Briggs shipyard), and Mast Landing.

The coming of the Kennebec & Portland Railroad to Freeport village in 1849 set the stage for the town's version of an industrial revolution, which took the form of shoe factories in the 1880s. The railroad was an important contributor to industrial development because it delivered coal for steam-powered factories and allowed transport of raw materials in and products out. Machinist Josiah Merrill was the first-known shop owner to employ steam power in the village, around 1880. Location of the rail line near the intersection of three vital roads—the County Road to Brunswick (Route 1), the road from Porter's Landing to Durham, and the stagecoach route along Pleasant Hill and Bow Street—solidified this area as an active crossroads of transportation by river, road, and rail. By its nature as a crossroads, the village with its heart at Freeport Corner has been defined by dramatic changes featuring buildings burned, moved, razed, and newly constructed. Fortunately, when Freeport celebrated its 100th anniversary in 1889, many of the prominent buildings in the village were photographed, thereby leaving a visual record of what stood at the time.

The first shoe shops were clustered in North Freeport in the area that bordered Durham's neighborhood known as "Shoetown," where nearly every household made shoes. Durham's industrial identity developed because of proximity to Auburn, the shoe-making capital of Maine, home to 21 large shoe-making factories. Martin V.B. Jordan produced the first case of shoes in Freeport in his shop on the Durham Road in 1869. A small factory operated by the Davis brothers on Beech Hill Road followed in 1872, which was active until they moved the business to Mechanic Street around 1881 and joined with S.E. Cushing. This began transformation of the village into a shoe-manufacturing mecca as village developer Edmund B. Mallet financed construction of two large steam-powered shoe factories, housing for shoe workers, and a gristmill and sawmill in the late 19th century. He also opened stores, a granite quarry, and brickyard, and invested in many other ventures. A.W. Shaw, H.E. Davis, Cumberland Shoe, Lenox Shoe, Freeport Shoe, E.E. Taylor, Free-Moc, L.L. Bean, and Eastland Shoe were some of the more than 30 different shoe manufacturers once located in Freeport. In the year 1957, the town had 10 factories employing about 1,000 people. Shoe manufacturing declined in the 1970s when production became less expensive overseas, and Eastland Shoe shipped the final case of Freeport-made shoes in 2001. A retail boom in the 1980s spearheaded by L.L. Bean and outlet stores reworked the village landscape.

This book follows an earlier version published more than 20 years ago, in 1996. Since then, the historical society's photographic collection has grown and our knowledge about what is shown in these images has expanded and been refined. *Freeport through the Years* represents an effort to highlight some recently found history as an addition to the important work that came before. While the general topics are similar—villages, people, homes, industry, businesses, community, pastimes, and transportation—much of what is described here is new.

Located adjacent to Gore's store, these buildings had multiple lives before and after they were moved. Here, Civil War veterans pose near a building that was originally constructed as a tin shop in 1847 by Harris and James Weeman. The Weemans made tinplates and stoves and, in 1861, sold the business to the Soules, who continued it as a shop and hardware store until it became the post office around 1885. Established in 1789, the village post office has been housed in several different locations over the course of its existence—near the Congregational church in 1857, at Main and School Streets in 1871, and in the Brewster and Holbrook Blocks in the 1890s. It moved to the Warren Block around 1900 and was located there until 1962, when a new building was constructed. The building on the right served as merchant Nathan Nye's and, later, E.B. Mallet's office. From 1878 to 1933, Charles Tuttle, Freeport's first and longest-running barber, set up shop in the building. The building on the left moved next to Harraseeket House and became incorporated into Mallet's Block in 1889, and the office building was moved to Bow Street where it continued as Tuttle's barbershop. It was razed in the 1980s for a retail block.

One

VILLAGES

This home at Kendall's Corner, built around 1820 by War of 1812 veteran Robert Kendall, had its original kitchen in the cellar. Known as Frost's Corner two centuries ago for early settler Phineas Frost, this intersection marks the northern boundary of Freeport Village. Located at a crossroads of travel to Durham or Brunswick, Samuel Hyde had a hatter's shop nearby from about 1810 to 1817. The Kendall family is seen playing croquet around 1880, before a second-story expansion was added to the house. (Courtesy of Lincoln Merrill Jr.)

Although Freeport's four villages have experienced major transformations in their multi-century history, no area has seen more rapid and dramatic changes than Freeport Corner. A transportation crossroads that included the commerce road between Durham and Porter's Landing, the original post road to Brunswick (Route 1), and the stagecoach route between Brunswick and Portland over Pleasant Hill—wagons, trolleys, and automobiles all converged at this location. Poignantly, everything in this view from near a century ago is now gone: from left to right, the Oxnard Block, Warren Block, and Smith (or Cates) Block, the trolley, a granite hitching post, and the town water hydrant. The Chinook husky drinking from the hydrant was named Semiluk; he was the lead dog in a sled team brought back from Greenland by famed Arctic explorer Donald MacMillan for local teenager Eddie Skillin. Cars passing this intersection became so numerous in the early 20th century that a stoplight was installed in 1937; it was removed after 1951 when the Freeport Bypass rerouted traffic. The Warren Block, L.L. Bean's longtime home, was built in 1894 by Orren W. Smith, whose middle name may have been Warren. It was razed in 1977 for L.L. Bean's expansion.

This building, shown in 1889, once sat on Main Street just north of Bow Street, an ideal commercial location for generations. Merchant Nathan Nye, who moved to Freeport in 1807, may have built the structure around 1820, since the store he owned with son-in-law Enoch Harrington was near this site. A variety of owners later kept stores here until the building was destroyed by fire in 1894, along with the adjacent Congregational church. It had previously been saved from burning when townspeople relayed buckets of water from a nearby well. Englishman Samuel Thing, an innholder in the 1840s, opened a store with Starrett Litchfield here in 1854. When Thing & Co. moved to the tavern across the square in 1860, merchants Creech & Means moved in until they sold to Jarvis A. Brewster, who owned the building when it burned. Before the fire, the block housed the post office, Golden Cross Hall, a barber, dentist, and dressmaker, as well as Brewster's store, which sold hardware, stoves, crockery, paint, and oil. Brewster later founded Casco Bay Packing Co., which processed clams at Porter's Landing.

Built in 1790 for Freeport's first minister, Thomas Means opened a tavern here around 1807, which was a stagecoach stop between Portland and Augusta. Samuel Holbrook used it as a store from 1815 until 1824, when Samuel Bliss again kept it as a tavern. Known as Holbrook Block by the 1870s, the structure housed many retail ventures until it was razed in the early 1970s. The building behind the stable may have been an early 19th-century store, and a shoe and cabinet-making shop around 1830. Holbrook and William Gore opened a store near the site of the building below at Main and Mechanic Streets in 1831, and the upstairs served as town meeting space. Although the structure was brick, it burned around 1844, destroying Masonic records. Gore & Holbrook rebuilt, and the new brick building shown below survived until the fire of 1909. Gore continued the store after Holbrook left in 1860, and from 1875 to 1889, partnered with William Davis to form Gore & Davis.

In 1888, Frederick Nichols built the Harraseeket House (above), a hotel with 25 rooms on the second and third floors, on a quarter acre of land he purchased in 1876 for $400. The block housed a hotel office, trolley waiting room, millinery, boot and shoe store, drugstore, and two grocery stores on the ground floor. A.W. Mitchell owned a stationery store and circulating library at the corner with 200 volumes of popular novels, magazines, and fashion books. Mallet constructed the adjacent block below in 1889. It housed a dry and fancy goods store and a general store, which was finished in polished whitewood and pine and had showcases and swinging stools advertised as "equal to those in any city." The emergence of these retail and service blocks reflected rapid growth caused by the village's industrial boom and foretold a surge of block building that would dramatically change the face of Freeport Village.

The home above was built around 1800 by mariner David Soule and was later owned by his son David B. Soule, a joiner. In 1857, merchant Robert S. Soule, son of prolific Porter's Landing shipbuilder Rufus Soule, purchased it and hired architect George Randall for renovations. Robert ran a packet boat between Freeport and Portland that supplied his village store from the 1820s until 1862, when he passed the business to his son Edward. A traveler in 1859 wrote that Soule's home was beautiful, "built in the imitation of a dark grey freestone and surrounded with an elegant iron fence," seen in the 1880s view above. The traveler was struck by the home's landscape, which had "an orchard with every tree pruned." The 1860 map below shows that apple orchards were a prominent feature of Main Street 150 years ago. The house was razed in 1973, and Key Bank replaced it.

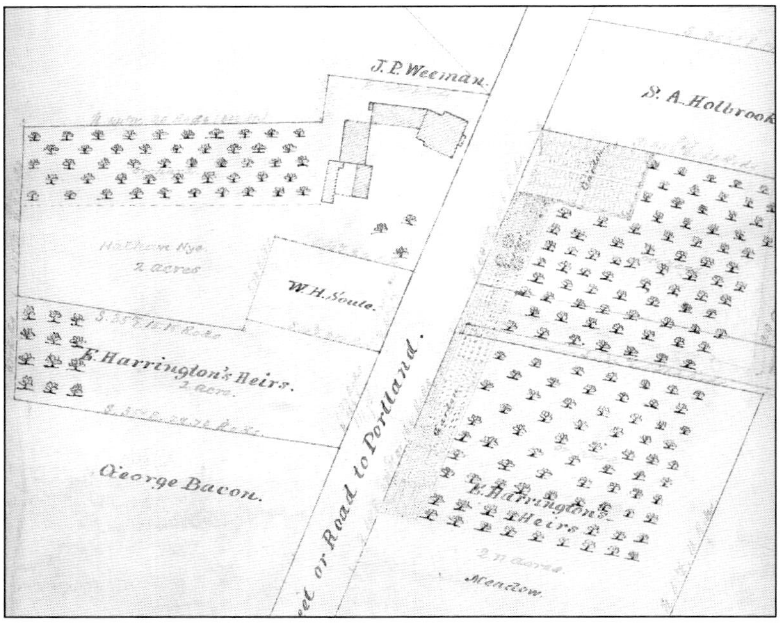

The connected buildings on Main Street at Mechanic Street above were the village's first business block, built around 1867 by Edward Oxnard with partner Washington Soule. Oxnard had 12 employees manufacturing clothing there in 1876, and 80 more working at home. Oxnard bought the property from Samuel Appleton Holbrook, who had a hall/arcade on Mechanic Street around 1852 that may have become the corner store, shown occupied by Stephen Mitchell around 1910. Its second floor and single story weathered a fire in 1915. Repairs were made, but in 1946, the block burned again, forcing it to be totally rebuilt. An 1889 view of the other end (below) shows Derosier's when it was a harness shop and housed surveyor E.C. Townsend's office, first dentist J.E. Harvey (note carved tooth sign), and homeopath Dr. Gannett. The building may have been Seth Bailey's store, adjacent to Gore's store around 1841 and moved down when the block was built.

Samuel Appleton Holbrook's home is shown with an elm tree uprooted by Hurricane Edna in 1954. Heir to his father's success in mercantile partnerships with Fowler, Clark, Hyde, and Gore, he continued in the business and became a community benefactor, building a hall/arcade on Mechanic Street around 1852 and donating a town park. Purchased by Eben Patterson, the home was razed in the 1960s and replaced by a retail block in 1983.

Cattle dealer Albert Kilby built this structure, once located across from the post office, as a cattle barn about 1913. Soon after, it became Longway's Garage, as seen here with, from left to right, Raymond Sears, Nevers Prosser, Arthur Bickford, and David Longway. The building remained a garage and gas station until Bond Wheelwright converted it into the Freeport, Maine, Country Store in 1969. These changes typified downtown development—retail replaced gas stations, which replaced husbandry and manufacture.

In 1909, a fire destroyed all the buildings between Bow and Mechanic Streets including the Mallet Block, which housed a brick bank and hardware store on the north corner (previously Gore & Davis store), Clark's Hotel, and the William Curtis residence on Bow Street. The only structure that survived was a small brick vault. In the image above, looking toward Mechanic Street, workers are cleaning up the destroyed area. The Davis Block was rebuilt as a brick structure the following year. The steam-powered pumper below was brought from Portland on a railroad car to help fight the fire. It is shown on Middle Street pumping from a town hydrant at the Bow Street corner in an attempt to save nearby buildings, such as the Cushing House at left. F.E. Merrill's printshop is in the background with the sign "Post Cards."

In the Main Street view above, the three houses at center are gone today. Joshua Mitchell's house (left), built around 1780, is the oldest remaining. Nathan Nye, a merchant from Sandwich, built the center-chimney house around 1847; it was razed in the 1940s to expand a gas station. Nye ran profitable stores in Freeport for about 60 years. The ladders were brought in to fight the block fire of 1909. Right of this view once sat the homestead of *Dash* commander George Bacon (below). A later resident, mariner John Oxnard, received restitution for a ship captured by the Confederates. Oxnard opened a store in 1856, purchased property, and accumulated wealth that passed to sons John and Edward, who built two business blocks in the village. Morse Street replaced the barn in 1922, and the house was razed in 1967 as L.L. Bean expanded.

Many buildings in Freeport Village, particularly the ones on Main Street, were moved, razed, or burned. Above, dairyman Edgar Conant is overseeing the move of this building down Bow Street to Carl Groves's lot near the railroad tracks in the 1930s. Buildings were often moved during winter months when snow and ice made a fine sliding surface. Groves used the structure as a shed, and the building is currently a commercial space at 25 Bow Street. The building below, once at the northeast corner of Main and Mechanic Streets, housed Freeport Hardware when it partially burned in a fire that started at the adjoining Roma Lunch in 1946. While townspeople watched, the building was saved by local firemen for the second time—the block also partially burned in 1915, causing the building to be remodeled narrower and with a flat roof.

Porter's Landing was an early deepwater port for shipbuilding, commerce, and transportation. Commercial buildings occupied the point, and a tidal sawmill near the bridge provided lumber for the shipyard (foreground and right) operated by Seward, William, and Samuel Porter. Cooper Samuel Lunt lived in the house at center, and Samuel Porter lived in the one at far left until around 1825, when he sold it to Rufus Soule, who took over the shipyard and went on to construct about 100 vessels with his son Rufus C. Soule.

The Porter's Landing schoolhouse, shown in 1885, was the second in the neighborhood. The first was located on Jacob Pettengill's land (east side of South Street) in the 1830s. The school was rebuilt on Lower Mast Landing Road in the 1860s. It was painted red in the 20th century and had wooden blackboards, a box stove, hooks for hanging mugs, a foot treadle organ, and cutout dolls decorating the room.

The channel at Porter's Landing was deep enough to accommodate vessels coming and going, although it required regular dredging to remain free of clay and silt. In 1894 and again in 1895, the channel was dredged 70 to 90 feet wide and 14 to 17 feet deep. The sediment was unloaded across the river near Wolfe's Neck in a location known as "the dump," which became a good place to dig clams.

The home of Joshua Soule, village shoemaker at Porter's Landing from about 1835 to the 1860s, overlooks a dammed pond where Abbot Weston harvested ice in the early 20th century. This area was developed as a saltworks in the 1780s, and also served as tanyards and powered a mid-19th-century tide mill. Shipwright Thomas Sylvester built the house at right around 1800; later, John Babson Lane, trader and shipwright, occupied it.

This portrait of Barnabas Bartol was painted in 1825 when he was 48 years old. His Bartol ancestors were from Salem, and his grandfather George Bartol (1721–1788) of Falmouth was the first of that surname to settle in Freeport. An early resident of Porter's Landing, George built a wharf and store and became a successful trader. So many Bartol descendants developed the area that it was known as Bartol's Landing by the mid-1800s. Barnabas's father, George Jr., served in the Revolution and survived the infamous Penobscot Expedition, earning the rank of captain for his bravery. Capt. George Bartol built the house below about 1770 on the hill above Porter's Landing. His daughter Phebe was living there with her husband, the Rev. Samuel Veazie, second minister of the Congregational church, when a fire in the home led to his death in 1809.

Charles Henry Pettengill and his wife, Phoebe Staples, of 56 South Street raised seven sons and one daughter, pictured above from left to right, (first row) Wallace Martin, Clara Cascolene holding photograph of Charles Augustus, Roscoe Irving, and Shirley Staples Pettengill; (second row) George Bartol, Alfred Henry, and Daniel Lane. Charles had a lucrative career shipping lumber along the coast, and also commanded vessels and owned a store at Porter's Landing. With his earnings, he bought homesteads for his sons including the one below across the road. Charles's father, Jacob, earlier owned the property and had established a schoolhouse on the lot before 1835. Barnabas Bartol constructed the home in 1808, and after a 1925 fire, it was remodeled to the one-and-a-half-story structure standing today. Pictured are Charles and Phoebe with their son George and his family, who occupied the homestead.

By 1910, South Freeport had emerged as a handsome village of houses built primarily by shipyard employees. Prior to the rise of shipbuilding around 1840, only a handful of families lived here, while more than 60 were settled by 1870. Early residents fished, farmed, and traveled by water since inland areas were not easily accessed until the 19th century. In 1799, residents petitioned for a road to the "best ship channel" in town, touting South Freeport's potential for shipping and shipbuilding and its close proximity to the river's mouth. Thomas Maines claimed the area in the 1730s, but before 1765, Falmouth wharf owner Christopher Strout recognized its promise and purchased the point that still bears his name. Casco Castle (above right and below), built 300 feet from Casco Bay's waters, offered "an unexcelled view in every direction" and brought tourism to the village.

This view of South Freeport from Casco Castle looking inland shows the grammar school (distant square building) and Congregational church (with bell tower) at left, built in 1884 after the original 1856 church burned. Three of six identical houses built for shipyard workers from 1851 to 1856 are shown (foreground right) facing Park Street, the only road laid out along the ancient range line defined by the town's proprietors in the 1730s.

When shipbuilding caused a population boom, South Freeport built a two-story grammar school in 1867 to accommodate 45 to 60 students. The older African American scholar may be Abraham Lincoln Spottswood, who moved to a waterfront home in 1909 that memorably hoisted a flag announcing independence. From Virginia, Spottswood was the first of 13 siblings born free to slave parents. He worked in a clothing store, and his son Stephen became a prominent minister.

South Freeport's store, built in 1854 by Samuel Osgood, also housed the village's first post office until 1972. Social events were held upstairs, and locals gathered daily at the hot stove to share stories and news. The Jones brothers, sons of ship carver Emery Jones, owned the store at the time of this c. 1900 photograph, and ran it for 47 years. The platform in front once served as a hay scales.

The small steamer *Corinna*, built in 1899 by the Portland, Freeport and Brunswick Steamboat Company, is shown unloading passengers at the steamboat landing in South Freeport around 1900, a time when industrial activity was quiet at the wharf. Following the demise of shipbuilding around 1880 and before Strouts Point became busy again during World War I, travelers rode steamers from here to the islands and accessed Casco Castle by steamboats that stopped here from 1903 to 1914.

Shipbuilding boosted the growth of South Freeport Village and sustained it for more than a century. Soule Brothers & Company, founded by brothers Enos, Henchman, and Clement, built about 30 vessels in its yard at Strouts Point from 1839 to 1879, and the nearby Bliss and Talbot yards built about 13 more. The industry slowed until Soule descendants formed Freeport Shipbuilding Company and received a government contract to build wooden Ferris-type steamers during World War I. Two were completed, and a third, the *Sintram*, was converted to a five-masted schooner when the war ended. The venture employed hundreds of men, shown above lined up along Main Street above the wharf in 1918. World War II brought a commission to the newly formed Casco Shipbuilding Company, which built four red-oak barges in the former Soule and Bliss yards, shown below. The track-like ways were constructed first and allowed completed vessels to slide into the water. (Below, courtesy of David Coffin.)

Lumbering was Freeport's first commercial activity, from around 1720 until harvesting shifted inland. Shipbuilding lumber flowed through town for two centuries, originally from Mast Landing where pine logs 80-plus feet long were dragged to the landing, floated downstream, and shipped to England for Royal Navy masts. The crew pictured above on Beech Hill Road around 1914 is logging with horses and oxen, a centuries-old practice. The view of Mast Landing below shows Daniel Curtis's general store (center), probably built around 1854, and later operated by David Osgood. Curtis's home (left) housed shipyard workers, and its ell may have served as Solomon Dennison's store from 1794 to 1845, followed by Cyrus Cole's store until 1853. Brickyard and wharf owners Joseph Lufkin, Joel Kelsey, and son John Kelsey also had a store in the building at right. Flat-bottomed gundalows rest on the site of a mid-century shipyard, located near a small building that was once the village schoolhouse.

In 1735, George Dennison of Gloucester purchased 800-plus acres of land in Freeport, most located near Mast Landing. Sons Abner and David moved to town in 1757 and built a sawmill, and later a gristmill, on their inherited land. By 1804, Abner's son Solomon had expanded the mill site to include a 30-foot dam, a four-story gristmill, a fulling mill with two carding machines, and a turning mill. The mills burned in 1861, but the impressive stone dam is still intact, as seen here near Gideon Dennison's home built on the hill about 1793. The road crossing the millstream to the left of the dam was washed out in 1956. (Courtesy of Donna J. Coffin.)

Fifteen local men repaired the bridge at Mast Landing after it was destroyed by heavy frosts in 1926. The cost was $2,024, which included construction of a temporary crossing. This bridge was worked on multiple times from when it was built in the 1780s to 1960, the last year it was repaired. Joseph Lufkin built the house above the river in 1795. Remains of a wharf are visible at right. It was used as a commercial dock for shipping bricks and mill products, and for receiving goods sold in the stores. (Courtesy of David Coffin.)

Robert Randall built this home around 1810; it was accessed by a road that once ran along Range D to Main Street, an earlier version of Upper Mast Landing Road. The home passed to son Daniel in 1849, the year the railroad came through their property. Walter Libby, whose son Greenlief made bricks at Mast Landing, purchased the house in 1862. He moved it closer to the landing, which is where it sat until its demise in 1967.

This house was constructed around 1815 by housewright Gideon Dennison Jr., who built several houses at Mast Landing. It remained in the Dennison family until 1905. Gideon was the nephew of Solomon Dennison, who sold house lots in the mill neighborhood to encourage development of a village. Two blacksmiths, Charles Stetson and Samuel Furbish, bought land and built houses around the same time, which shows the importance of their trade to early villages.

Two

People and Homes

In 1877, the Pettengills purchased the homestead known as Pettengill Farm and farmed the land for over 80 years. Ancestor Abraham Pettengill came to the area from Salisbury in 1730, and his descendants developed farms around the Harraseeket estuary. Frank and sister Mildred Pettengill (pictured) worked the land as a dairy from 1925 until 1959. They lived in the farmhouse without any running water, electricity, or central heating into their 80s.

Wallace Pettengill, shown above with his dairy cows, ran Pettengill farm with his children Frank and Mildred until he died in 1925. They milked 8 to 12 cows by hand and sold their cream and homemade butter locally. The milk was carted by wagon to Freeport Village where it was then transported by railroad to Portland and sold to Hood Dairy or Old Tavern Farm. In addition to milk cows, the Pettengills had pigs, geese, horses, ducks, chickens, an apple orchard, and large vegetable and flower gardens. Frank Pettengill (below) mowed the hay fields by horse-drawn mower through the 1950s when others were using tractors. He cut ice on a small pond near their home to keep milk cold and did the heavy farm labor, while Millie tended the gardens and prepared food, including canning clams she dug from the flats.

The Pettengill farmhouse was built or expanded in the 1790s by mariner Aaron Lufkin, who brought the saltbox-building tradition from his native Gloucester. He started a brickyard and probably built the large wharf that partially remains to load finished bricks for transport. The 35-by-40-foot English barn at right above collapsed in the late 1950s, and the privy shed and other original outbuildings are also gone, though some have been rebuilt. The barn may have been built by the Rodick family who began saltwater farming here in the 1830s. The property retains features used to harvest salt hay, such as dykes, sluice gates, and staddles. An unidentified presumed seaman etched drawings of several War of 1812 frigates into the upstairs walls of the farmhouse. The "sgraffiti" below is labeled "LARNC," which may be a phonetic spelling referring to James Lawrence, captain of the USS *Chesapeake* on which he died in 1813.

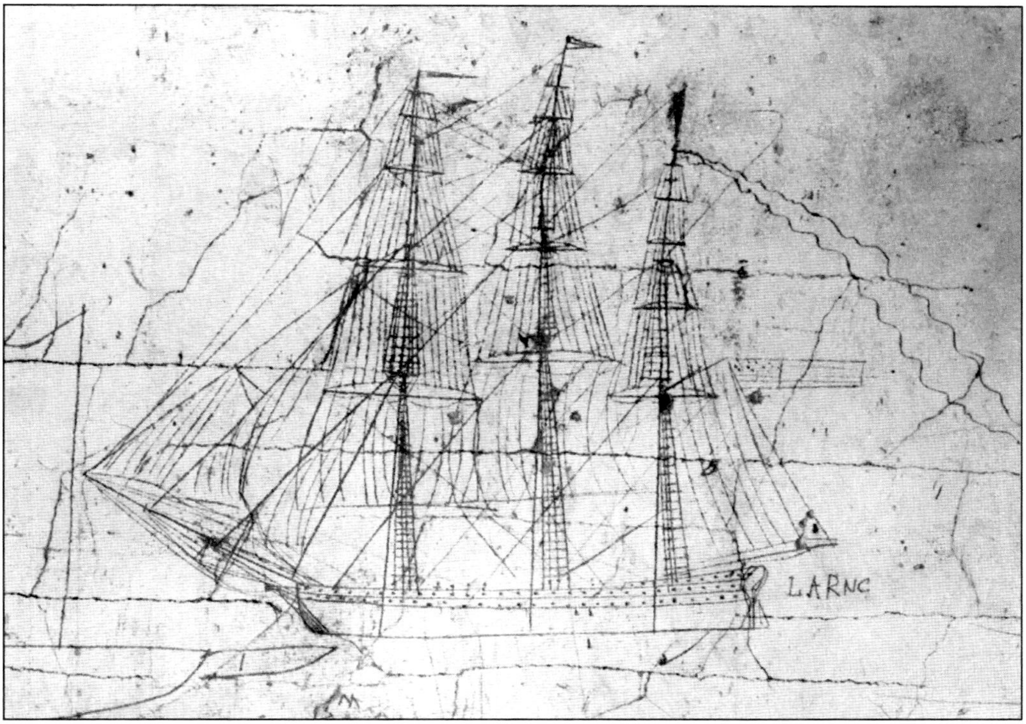

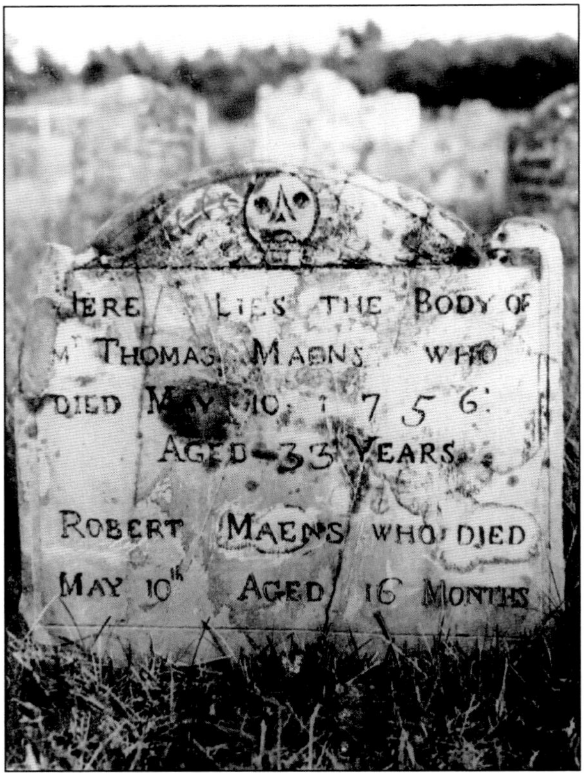

On May 10, 1756, Native Americans attacked the Scots-Irish Means family living on Flying Point. Thomas Means and his young son Robert were killed; his wife, Alice, was wounded; and her sister Molly Finney was carried to Quebec. Two other children escaped by hiding. The dead were buried in Brunswick's First Parish Cemetery beneath this gravestone with the Puritan "death's head," a symbol that represented the mortality of the body and immortality of the soul. Although the attack involved only two deaths, it became known as the "Means Massacre," a story that was retold over the years as a reminder of the dangers early settlers faced. Before an audience of 700-plus people, a 1932 reenactment of the event was staged at the site by descendants of the original family, including, from left to right, (first row) children Hilda Coffin and Dorothy Mann; (second row) Marietta Coffin, Horace Mann, and baby Kenneth Fourier.

In 18th-century Freeport, blockhouses or garrisons were built to protect settlers from Native American attacks, which were still common during the resettlement period starting around 1720. These thick-walled buildings were constructed of hewn logs to slow bullets, often included a second-story overhang, and sometimes had palisades. This house off Bartol Island Road, built by George Bartol and razed about 1934, was known locally as a garrison and may have billeted British soldiers who oversaw lumbering at Mast Landing. The blockhouse on Flying Point was built to protect the Scots-Irish Anderson, Mann, Means, Rogers, Patten, and Spear families who originally purchased land from the Dummer claim. Thomas Mann (pictured with his family below), descendant of settler Gideon Mann, was a Civil War veteran, stonemason, and ship carpenter. From left to right are his wife, Hannah; Thomas; and their children Lida, Eva, and Horace at their homestead on Wolfe's Neck. (Below, courtesy of John Mann.)

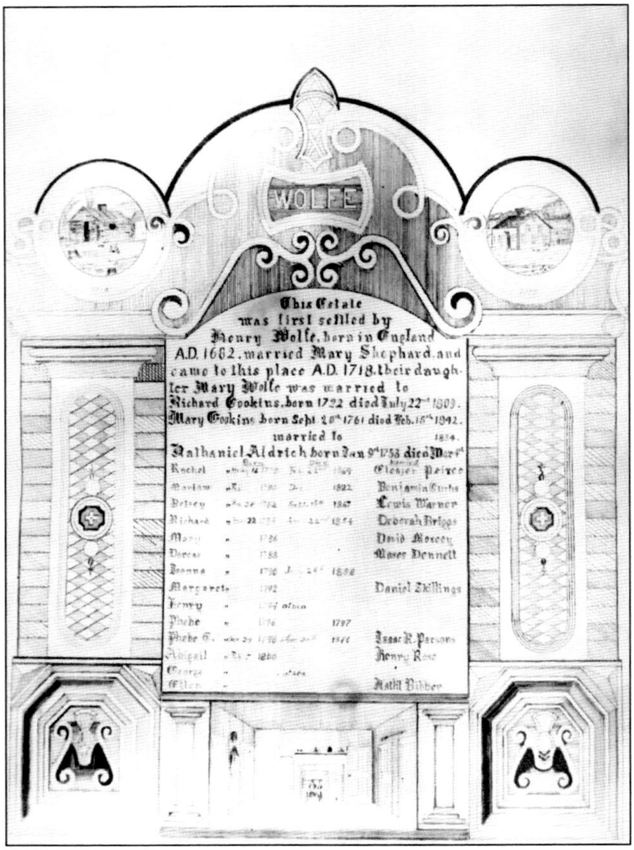

The illustrated genealogy at left shows the early settlers of Wolfe's Neck and the origin of its name. Originally called Shephard's Point after Thomas and Anne Shephard, who settled there in 1666 but were driven away by Native Americans, the land was reclaimed by Englishman Henry Wolfe when he married a Shephard daughter or granddaughter, either Mary, as shown here, or Rachel, according to other records. Wolfe built a log cabin and planted an orchard in 1718 (inset upper left), and descendants Gookins or Aldrich built the frame house (right) in 1777. The property stayed in the family for seven generations until it was sold to E.B. Mallet in 1888. Soon after, Mallet built a large hay barn, shown below. The farmstead to the right may include some of the original settlers' buildings, since the structure next to the barn dates to the mid- to late 18th century.

Mariner Greenfield Pote built the saltbox house above around 1760 near Waite's Landing in Falmouth. When his wife died, Pote married a widow from Freeport and moved his house by water to its current location on Wolfe's Neck in 1787. Local lore contends that this dramatic act was precipitated by a fine Pote received for sailing on the Sabbath, but historical records do not support this. Instead, the move was more likely related to his second marriage and economic opportunity on the Harraseeket River, where he built a tide mill and wharf. Greenfield's son William probably built the central part of the large barn, and both father and son are buried at the fenced-in Pote cemetery at left. The men below are standing at the location of Pote's wharf in 1902 with South Freeport in the distance. (Below, courtesy of the Maine Historic Preservation Commission.)

E.B. Mallet, shown at left in his Knights of Pythias uniform, inherited a large sum of money and used it to develop Freeport Village. From 1886 to the 1890s, he built shoe factories, a sawmill and gristmill, and housing for workers, and opened a store, brickyard, and granite quarries. Architect Francis Fassett designed the house below for Mallet at 184 Lower Main Street in 1887; today, the property looks similar, sans windmill. It once had a billiard hall left of the barn that was moved farther south in 1924, converted into a house, and later razed. Following separation from his wife, Clara, Mallet purchased and moved to the adjacent home, which may have been built around 1800 by Daniel Cummings, a joiner who also constructed the first Baptist church in town. As a member of the Maine senate, Mallet supported women's suffrage in municipal elections in 1893, although the bill failed.

Mallet built this granite pier at the end of Wolfe's Neck about 1890 for shipping hay to the thousands of horses pulling carriages in Philadelphia, New York, and Boston. The hay was cut on his newly acquired 291 acres of land that extended from Little River to the point and was stored in his unusually large 45-by-100-foot barn, which still stands today. The moored boat is the *Heyden* of Little Bustins.

The barkentine *Kingdom*, shown in Harraseeket Bay, was purchased in 1906 by Rev. Frank Sandford, leader of Durham's evangelical Holy Ghost and Us Church, or "Shiloh." Sandford sailed with church members from Wolfe's Neck pier to Jerusalem, the Caribbean, Africa, and Greenland before the vessel ran aground in 1911. When 66 stranded crew members boarded the companion *Coronet*, overcrowding led to six deaths by scurvy. Sandford was indicted for manslaughter and served seven years in prison.

The Dennison family of Gloucester, Massachusetts, first came to Freeport in the 1750s when patriarch George bequeathed 800-plus acres of land he had acquired to his seven children. Descendants spread throughout town and proved themselves adept entrepreneurs, inventors, and military leaders. Aaron Lufkin Dennison (pictured), born in Freeport in 1812, was the first to mechanize the manufacture of watch parts, which earned him the legacy of "father of the watchmaking industry."

Appleton Webster, cousin to S.A. Holbrook, was a brick mason from Yarmouth who came to Freeport around 1853 and moved to this home at 49 West Street around 1866. The house was built around 1770, probably on Main Street, and was moved to this location before 1871. Sons Frank and George worked for the railroad, and one of them may be shown here (left) with his family. Their mother, Lydia, lived here with daughter Nellie until her death.

The son of a prominent lawyer, Josiah Mitchell was born in the house above on Upper Main Street in 1813. He became a respected sea captain and was known for surviving a harrowing experience. On May 3, 1866, the ship he commanded, the *Hornet*, accidentally caught fire and burned at sea off the western coast of South America. The crew escaped into three lifeboats, but with only 10 days' rations. At the mercy of wind and weather, they eventually separated the tethered boats, and only the largest boat, carrying Mitchell and 13 others, made it to Hawaii 43 days and 4,300 miles later. Two of the survivors were brothers Henry and Samuel Ferguson, ages 18 and 28, who were traveling to San Francisco; their diaries recount starvation and near mutiny. A painting of the disaster commissioned by a Ferguson descendant in 1927 is shown below. (Above, courtesy of Judith Elfring.)

Built by joiner Joseph Mitchell around 1780, this house at 21 Main Street was the longtime residence of Dr. John Angier Hyde, Freeport's first physician, who practiced for 65 years from 1792 to 1857. Born in Rehoboth, Massachusetts, Hyde studied with a Boston physician before moving to the Elisha Torrey house near the original Congregational meetinghouse. For a short time, he lived in the Jameson-Codman Tavern, built around 1797 by Jonathan Cushing. Son Ephraim Hyde and grandson Nathan Hyde also became doctors, while daughter Mary wed town doctor Ebenezer Wells. The Wellses lived at Main at School Streets, where he was the postmaster for 20 years. They later moved to the brick home at 39 Main Street. The 1890s interior view below shows it was opulently finished and furnished, consistent with its occupation by sea captains, shipbuilders, and doctors, including Henchman Soule and Dr. Harvey Howard.

After starting his career in Kennebunk, Dr. David Dana Spear (1839–1899) practiced medicine in Freeport for most of his professional life, from 1873 until 1897. He made house calls, dispensed medicines, and delivered babies, often collecting his medical fee in trade for food, goods, or services. During his 24 years in town, he oversaw 645 "obstetrical cases," charging between $8 to $10 for normal deliveries and up to $40 for those with complications.

This building is well-known to Freeport residents as the hospital where Drs. Harvey Howard and Arthur Gould saw patients and delivered babies from 1926 to 1941. Built about 1890 on land that was once Enoch Harrington's apple orchard, the building served as a private residence before and after it was a hospital. It was razed in the 1980s to make way for a retail block.

Percy C. Pratt (center) was known for writing poetry that provided local news to 450 Freeport men serving overseas during World War II. Between 1942 and 1945, Pratt mailed out 150 editions of his newsletter, which told Freeport news in rhyme. In 1968, the mason-shipyard-worker-turned-postal-clerk compiled his writings into a book, *On the Square*. Notably, Pratt built seven homes after retirement, working into his late 80s.

John T. Gould (right), posing with siblings at their Maple Avenue home around 1920, grew up to be a well-known author. He published popular articles about Freeport and Maine, often satirical and historically based. In 1942, Gould began a weekly column for the *Christian Science Monitor* that continued for 50-plus years. Gov. Angus King founded "John Gould Day" on August 17, 2002, to recognize the writer's success capturing Maine's "unique character and language."

Abraham Mitchell was an early settler of Porter's Landing, known as Mitchell's Landing before the 1790s. He served in the French and Indian War in 1758 and worked transporting goods on the river by gundalow, a flat-bottomed boat. Sometime after buying the land in 1768, he built the house above at the end of Varney Road. The house originally faced the water, as shown here, and was accessed from South Street. What is now Varney Road was built for travel to the meetinghouse about 1790. In 1825, the homestead was sold to Barnabas and Mary Carver, who hired a folk artist to paint portraits of the family including the one at right of their daughter Frances—their only child to survive toddlerhood—around 1835. In the early 20th century, Ernest Varney enlarged the home to a two-story hip-roof structure. (Right, courtesy of the American Folk Art Museum.)

Ellen Ballard, the daughter of shipmaster Justus Richardson of Mast Landing, came naturally to life at sea. After her marriage to Capt. James Ballard, she often accompanied him to faraway ports. Recognizing the danger of ocean travel, Ellen asked her husband's promise that she would never be buried at sea. When she became ill and died aboard the *Lucille* en route to Japan, the captain staged a mock burial to assuage the superstitious crew and secretly kept her body in a brine-filled lead casket, eventually bringing her home to be buried in Freeport. For many years, Ballard captained the well-known ship the *Tam O'Shanter II*, built in 1875 at the Soule yard. The *Tam*, shown below moored in New York City, was an exceptionally fast clipper ship that famously won a race around Cape Horn by only two hours. (Left, courtesy of David Coffin; below, courtesy of Peabody Essex Museum.)

James Small moved to Freeport from Bowdoinham in 1857 and, soon after, married resident Mary Jane Curtis. They raised five children at their home off Pleasant Hill Road, which is where James and Mary celebrated their 50th wedding anniversary in 1907, pictured above. The house was struck by lightning and burned some years later. In 1902, their son Walter became one of Freeport's first Rural Free Delivery (RFD) mail carriers, a system funded by the Federal government as a result of lobbying by the National Grange. Since farmers generally lived far from villages and could not easily pick up their mail, RFD was a fitting cause for the pro-agriculture organization. Consistent with Grange ideals that valued the work of men and women, both genders were hired as mail carriers. Walter, shown below delivering mail in his wagon pulled by Molly, often shared his job with daughter Lida. (Both, courtesy of Lincoln Merrill Jr.)

Local artist James Lane Berkeley, trained in design, ran a four-week summer camp for children in the 1940s. His brochure included photographs showing campers at the Lane family's homestead on Pleasant Hill Road (left). The camp cost $10 per week and included farm-cooked meals, music and stories, building projects, and berry picking. The Lane house was built about 1780 by Berkeley's ancestor Thomas Bicknell, and it stayed in the family until 2009. According to family lore, the large elm in this c. 1900 photograph was brought from Connecticut in a flowerpot. The Lanes were descendants of early settler James Lane who built a farmstead on Foggs Point and owned Lane's Island in the 17th century. He was killed during the Indian Wars, and his family fled to Gloucester, but descendants later reclaimed the land and resettled in Freeport.

Noah Pratt came to Freeport from Abington with his father in-law, Thomas Bicknell, around 1780. Together, they owned the Pleasant Hill Road farmstead shown on the opposite page. Pratt lived there for a decade while developing his stonecutting business, a profession shared with his father, two brothers, and a son. His unique style of portrait art is recognizable on the 40-plus stones he carved in Freeport, such as this one at Mast Landing Cemetery.

Sadie and William Ringrose, a sailor from England, came to Freeport about 1850 and settled off Pleasant Hill Road. Their daughter Etta is shown (right) at the Ringrose homestead with aunt Mart Ringrose (left) and child Alice about 1900. Etta married Elmer Welch, a canned-goods merchant who later worked as a repairman at the electric carbarn. Alice grew up to marry Charles Hilton, who owned a crabmeat factory at Porter's Landing.

Born into a Porter's Landing family with siblings Archella, Ganzella, Rosilla, and Electus, George Wiltshire Randall perhaps knew himself unique. He became a house and ship joiner and designed a number of homes in Freeport. Serving as captain in the Civil War for the 25th and 30th Maine Regiments, Randall was promoted to brigadier general for bravery. He is shown second from right near his officer's tent. Freeport's Grand Army of the Republic (GAR) post was renamed for him following his death in 1897. The Randall-designed house below, surrounded by a handsome lathe-turned fence, was built for stevedore Benjamin Dennison about 1856. Merchant Gershom Bliss also lived here, as did the Josiah and Emilie Soule family beginning in 1874 until it burned in the early 1900s. At the time of this 1890s photograph, daughter Ellen and Willis Soule were living in the home.

Barnabas Soule, a *Mayflower* descendant from Duxbury, settled on the Cousins River in the 1740s. Son Barnabas served in the Revolution and built this homestead on the "Neck" (Lambert Road) about 1775, where he farmed and had 12 children with his wife, Jane Dennison. Several sons engaged in the shipping industry, including Enos, Henchman, and Clement, who founded the Soule Shipyard in South Freeport. Enos lived here in his later years.

This house at 18 Main Street in South Freeport was built around 1853 by ship carpenter Benjamin P. Soule, who worked at the Soule Brothers & Company's shipyard. He is seen here at left with a horse and his family about 1885. His wife, Almira, is second from right, and daughter Georgianna is center left. Georgianna married William Stockbridge, a Civil War veteran, professional singer, and music teacher. He died tragically in 1903, crushed between two freight cars while running to catch a train.

In 1800, Perez Burr started a shoe-making business on Route 136. The company was passed on to son Perez and continued for seven decades. Burr was a master shoemaker who taught the Davis brothers, founders of their own shoe-making dynasty. In 1871, the Burrs built greenhouses that were heated by the steam-powered shoe-making infrastructure. Shown with their 25-year-old rosebush, grandson John (right) and his son Perez operated a floral business there until 1946.

Around 1923, Edward "Bumpy" Hayes moved to Freeport from Lewiston-Auburn and served as station agent for 20 years. Shown in a rare interior view of the depot office, Hayes was a 50-year employee of the Maine Central Railroad and chairman of the Railroad Telegraphers Union for years, beginning in 1915. He traveled widely in the United States, Canada, and Mexico, and ran for representative to the Maine legislature in the 1930s but did not win. (Courtesy of Nancy Sulides.)

Enabled by her family's prosperity, Claire Soule, the daughter of Susan and capitalist George W. Soule, was a talented artist who made a career of painting still lifes, landscapes, and portraits, an unusual path for a woman at the time. Claire is shown working on the portrait of her cousin Margaret Soule Wengren, daughter of shipyard mogul Enos Soule, about 1900. Claire married William Sprague in her 50s and never had children.

Photographer F.E. Merrill started Freeport Press, the first printing press in town, about 1889. He used it to print the *Freeport Sentinel* and postcards in his shop on Middle Street. The press later moved to the second floor of the Warren Block where Helen Randall ran it from 1915 to 1934. She printed L.L. Bean's first flyer and early catalogs on the press shown in this 1920s photograph with worker Lottie Brown Libby.

Isaac Skillin is shown on the frozen Harraseeket River with Earle Litchfield posed on a piling, an Arctic husky dog, and a Model B Ford. "Ike" borrowed the vehicle from MacMillan's engineer John Jaynes and drove it to Bustins Island from South Freeport in February 1932. Skillin parked the car at his friend's cottage on the island and walked home across the ice, leaving the automobile stranded for months. (Courtesy of John W. Skillin.)

The Randall family is shown with friends on a summer outing around 1900. Helen Randall (back row, seated second from right) was a portrait artist. Her father, Rufus, was a prosperous sea captain who had eight children with his wife, Annie, three of whom were born at sea. Rufus Randall became a cabin boy at 11 and shipmaster at 25, commanding vessels, like the Freeport-built *John A. Briggs*, around the world. Family friend Donald MacMillan is at far left.

Famed Arctic explorer Donald MacMillan attended Freeport High School after relocating from Provincetown to live with older sister Letitia following the death of his parents. A member of the supply team that helped Admiral Peary reach the North Pole in 1909, MacMillan ("Mac") continued to explore polar regions as his life's work on the specially outfitted schooner *Bowdoin*. Crewmates, from left to right, John Jaynes (engineer), Tom Mix (radio operator), Captain Mac, Jot Small (cook), and Tom McCue (mate) pose in the 1930s. McCue was a colorful mariner who worked as a fisherman and later captained a rum-running vessel. Mac brought a number of Arctic animals home to Maine for his studies, and some, such as the Chinook huskies and foxes, became pets for friends. The blue fox chained on the *Bowdoin* (below) looks longingly at the sea, seemingly too wild to become domestic.

Simeon Coffin had a carriage-making shop at Main and West Streets near an early town pound. His homestead was part of the ministerial lot purchased from Reverend Merrill in 1829. Simeon's apple orchard beyond the family graveyard became Woodlawn Cemetery in 1857. Son Llewellyn (right), shown in 1887 with his family at their home on West Street, was a shipbuilder and also made coffins and carriages. E.B. Mallet's houses are in the distance.

Clifford "Mel" Collins studied at the New York Institute of Photography and worked as a photographer for L.L. Bean and for the *Brunswick Record*. From a musical family, Collins played clarinet in the Freeport Marching Band. He also played bass with the Maine Mountaineers, shown here in 1939. Because of his commitment to collecting and recording historical images, the historical society created the Mel Collins Volunteer Award in 1993.

Fred P. Davis started farming on South Freeport Road near Grover's Crossing about 1880. Son Fred L. built a house across the road around 1902 and used his fields for raising ducks. The Davis Duck Plant in this 1910 postcard view shows his parents' house in the distance. The card is written to Mrs. Edgar Curtis offering to pay 14¢ per pound for ducks over five pounds. Davis opened a baby chick hatchery around 1932 and ran it until 1959. Another poultry breeder, Fred H. Goldrup, raised fancy chickens for Freeport Poultry Association competitions from 1908 to 1917. Shown around 1910 with his prize chicken, Fred and his wife, Lillian, worked as cutter and stitcher in a shoe factory. They were the first employees hired by L.L. Bean to work at night making Bean boots, just as Mallet hired Goldrup's father, John, as his quarry's first foreman.

Marcellus Coffin and Susie Clough lived on Bartol Island Road in this house he built about 1871 after buying the land from his brother Otis L. Coffin, a Civil War veteran who lived to be 100 years old. Descendants of early settlers Abner and Mary Coffin, the brothers were handy woodworkers. After the war, Otis purchased this property where he cut trees and may have fashioned the bench-desks for the Porter's Landing School, built around 1866.

James Coffin inherited this donkey from "Daddy Jim" Coombs, a vaudeville actor who lived above the millsite. Coffin tried to coax "Mickey" into hauling wood and hay, but he often refused, as shown in this photograph of him parked in the road. Mickey was terrified of thunderstorms, so Vera Coffin tied him to the cookstove in the house to keep him calm. He capitalized on her kindness by stealing pies cooling on the windowsill. (Courtesy of David Coffin.)

Three

Industry and Businesses

The arrival of the railroad in 1849 revolutionized industry in Freeport. This c. 1890 view shows the pockets (right) where coal for locomotives was unloaded into a large pit and hauled from there to engine houses. Even before E.B. Mallet transformed the village into an industrial center, Soule Brothers & Company developed the coal market. Mallet's square office (center) and his worker-built houses (left) are all that remain.

By the time of the 1887 map below, Mallet had developed a gristmill, shoe factory, granite quarry, and brickyard. A monument shop, sawmill, lumberyard, coal pockets, another shoe factory, business block with stores, and 180 worker houses came in subsequent years. The c. 1890 view of the village above shows the shoe factory (right), monument shop (left), mills and depot (center), and brickyard in the foreground, which produced a million bricks per year. In 1886, the yard fired 240,000 bricks in a single day—a process that required eight days of burning. Earlier in the century, brickyards were prevalent on the river, where clay and sand were readily available. Mast Landing, Porter's Landing, Flying Point, and Wolfe's Neck had yards that transported bricks by boat. Kelseys, Lapham, Fogg, Brewers, Mann, Wilbur, Collins, Dunning, and Rogers fired 160,000–500,000 bricks per year from the 1850s to the 1870s.

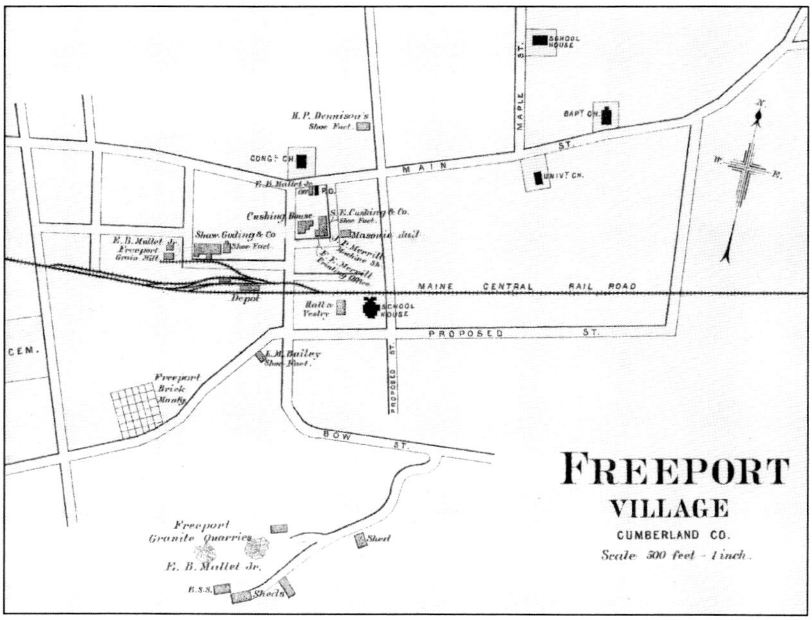

Shoe making became an important industry after shipbuilding declined, and was prolific for more than a century. In 1886, Mallet built this large factory, originally occupied by A.W. Shaw, which boasted Freeport's first telephone in 1893. The building later housed Cumberland Shoe, Lenox, Sears & Roebuck, Porter & Sons, Sawyer Boot & Shoe, E.E. Taylor, and Loree Shoe. Men and women worked on separate floors as stitchers, cutters, bottomers, or lasters.

This rare interior photograph of the A.W. Shaw shoe factory shows women in the stitching room about 1910. From left to right are (first row) Isabelle Miller, Jeanette Allen, Ruth Kelly, and Evelyn Sawyer; (second row) Mrs. Charles Miller, Mrs. William Royal, Mrs. Leon Britt, and Mrs. Willard Butterfield. Presumably the married women were the younger women's mentors. Jeanette Allen was a stitcher all her life and married Harry Byram, a ship joiner. (Courtesy of Kevin Byram.)

The building above, once located on Mechanic Street, was the first steam-powered shoe factory in the village, a venture between S.E. Cushing and the Davis brothers, who began manufacturing on Beech Hill Road in 1872. The factory operated from 1881 until 1898, when H.E. Davis reorganized and moved to a larger facility on West Street. The building was used for storage until the Small-Abbott Shoe Company, started by Clarence Small, son Frank, and Edward Abbott, revived manufacturing there in 1927 and made moccasins on-site for the next three decades. Decline of the shoe-making industry led to its razing around 1980. Clarence Small; his wife, Bertha; and their children are pictured below at the railroad station around 1911. Behind the factory was J.P. Merrill's machine shop, where tools were made on a foot-powered lathe beginning in 1866. Merrill later manufactured shoe-making knives using steam power until 1918. (Below, courtesy of Elinor Hudson.)

H.E. Davis & Co. moved its shoe-making operation to this Mallet-built factory on West Street around 1898, the site of Freeport's first dynamo for commercial lighting. The factory employed 175 hands compared to 100 working at the Shaw factory, which illustrates the immense size of the building. Davis installed the latest manufacturing equipment, rebuilt the steam system, and produced millions of women's shoes and boots until the 1960s. Overhead shafts with belts driving the machinery ran the length of the building. The only surviving shoe manufacturing facility, the building currently houses L.L. Bean's warehouse and employee store. Over the course of 100 years, Davis Shoe was one of about 30 different companies that made shoes in Freeport. In 1957, the town had 10 factories employing about 1,000 people. In the photograph below, workers at A.W. Shaw pose outside the factory in work aprons.

In the early 20th century, the legend of the "Vanishing Indian" led to the popularity of "Indian-style" moccasins. Capitalizing on this interest, Freeport manufacturers L.L. Bean and Small-Abbott began producing handmade moccasins in the 1930s, followed by Totem Moc, Village Shoemaker, and Casco Bay Moc in the 1950s and 1960s. The latter made shoes for customers as they watched. Roland Houle is shown hand-sewing a moccasin at L.L. Bean in the early 1950s.

Julian Leslie erected the "Big Indian" in 1969 to draw attention to his Casco Bay Trading Post, which specialized in moccasins hand-stitched on site. "Chief Passamaquoddy" is made of painted fiberglass, weighs over a ton, and stands 30 feet high. Built by an Amish artisan in Pennsylvania at a cost of $7,200, it was trucked to Route 1 where it has stood as a Freeport landmark for nearly 50 years.

Shown above on opening day, June 13, 1897, Freeport House was a guesthouse expanded from a home on Park Street. Frank Libby, and later, Fred Ward, served as proprietors. Travelers with the shoe industry, baseball teams, and theater and concert groups boarded here. The building later returned to private housing until it was razed in 1984. George Parker established an earlier Freeport House in the original Oxnard-Soule Block around 1875. Warren Harlow, proprietor of a summer hotel on Peaks Island, continued it as a guesthouse and restaurant from 1888 to 1897. The Harraseeket House opened in 1888, and Abbie Cushing and Sarah Chase also operated boardinghouses in the period between 1890 and 1924. The shoe factory boom created so much demand for living space that many residents housed factory workers. Alfred Bisbee's barn on West Street (below) was divided into tenement apartments and became known as "Harmony Hall" in the 1930s.

Mallet's monument shop was a semicircular building that formed a working dooryard where stones were loaded and unloaded onto and from railroad cars using a derrick. Built around 1889, the stoneworks produced all kinds of rock monuments—bases, shafts, sarcophagi, plinths, dies, and caps. Finished examples are visible at right. Stones were cut and processed by 50 skilled workmen under superintendent George Lovell. A polishing shop behind the monument shed used steam-powered tools to shape and polish local granite and marble brought in by train. The quarry and monument shop also employed blacksmiths, shown in the view below looking toward Bisbee's house and barn on West Street. John Stowell (left rear) and cutter Irving Morse are in the photograph. Mallet's stoneworks used 100 men, 12 horses, and 6 oxen in 1889, and these numbers were expected to double to meet orders the following year.

The c. 1895 view down Mill Street above shows Mallet's sawmill in the foreground (right) and lumberyard (left) with the shoe factory behind. In the distance, the furnace (with chimney) generated steam power for the sawmill and gristmill beyond. Mallet sold his industries to other businessmen after a few years. E.C. Hyde ground 1,000 bushels of grain per week from 1893 to 1895, followed by J.C. and Olin Clark, who ran the gristmill until about 1920, when the Farmer's Union took over. Starting around 1933, Freeport Grain Company occupied the buildings, which burned in 1971. From 1898 to 1913, Edward Libby ran Mallet's wooden box factory and sawmill, making boxes for shoes, corn, and fish and cutting five million feet of lumber per year. Below, sawmill employees take a break on Oak Street. By 1912, production had slowed, and later moved to a smaller structure, while auto painting occupied the original mill building.

Mechanic Street had two carriage painting shops, one behind Gore's store where William Curtis worked from about 1880 to 1896, and this carriage-making and paint shop next to the Masonic hall. Owned by Stilkey brothers James (left) and Charles (right) from about 1890 to 1920, the shop is shown in 1898 with Mr. Soule and Presbury Dennison on the second floor. Later, the building became a house and then the Corsican restaurant, which burned in 2016.

Albion Woodman and Charles Wyman built this structure on School Street around 1895 to house their carriage repair and upholstery shop. The structure at right served as lumber storage. Carpenter Elmer L. Porter bought the business in 1915 and operated a lumberyard here for years, which was continued by son Elmer Jr. as Freeport Building Supplies until 1978. Elmer Sr. built the hose tower, Bustins Island cottages, and many Freeport houses and barns.

The building at 25 Lunt Road was constructed by Silas and Henry Goddard around 1810 as a mill to manufacture the Goddard plow, advertised as the "best turning plow you ever saw." The millworks, shown here with Victor Coffin, remained in the building until it became a private home in 1972. Power for the vertical saw and lathes on the second floor came from this sweep, powered by horses. (Courtesy of David Coffin.)

This is the only known photograph of a mill in Freeport, the old Wardtown sawmill on Royal River's East Branch near Durham-Brunswick. The century-old mill was no longer operational by the time this c. 1890 photograph was taken by Annie May Collins. Another sawmill and gristmill were located farther downstream near the Route 136 crossing. Annie was the sister of violin maker, music teacher, and barber Melvin T. Collins.

The U-shaped ribs for the hulls of the Ferris-type steamers built during World War I in South Freeport were constructed on the ground, as shown above at the old Bliss yard around 1918. The completed ribs were then hoisted with pulleys to their position on the stocks. At left, the size of the rudder of a red-oak barge under construction around 1943 is apparent relative to the men attaching it. Roman numerals on the stern are for determining the ship's weight with and without cargo. (Left, courtesy of David Coffin.)

The scene above shows the launching of the first South Freeport–built barge, *Red Oak I*, in April 1943. Construction of the vessel, which was 134 feet long, took about nine months, and all the lumber was cut in Maine. The public event was attended by hundreds of people, including Gov. Sumner Sewall. Strouts Point Wharf Company constructed the building at center in 1831, and it served multiple purposes over its 175-plus-year lifetime, including housing Casco Yacht Club. The last surviving remnant of a proud shipbuilding era, it was moved to a private home in 2008. On the Harraseeket River just after launching in June 1943, *Red Oak II* is shown below pulled by a tugboat as well-wishers wave and cheer. The barges were made of wood to prevent detection by land mines and were built without self-propulsion to allow maximum space for hauling supplies. (Above, courtesy of David Coffin.)

Originally known as Griffin's Point, and later Weston's Point, a road extended from here to Route 1 around 1770, marking this area as one of early settlement. The site of Cushing-Briggs shipyard from 1855 to 1880, the building shown above served as the yard's sawmill. Here, master shipbuilder George Anderson built 11 wooden sailing vessels, so well-constructed that many survived the days of sailing vessels to become coal barges. Anderson, the grandson of Means Massacre survivor Jane Means, designed his first vessel for shipbuilder Capt. Enoch Talbot. This area became a summer cottage community around 1900, and little remains of its shipbuilding past. Fishermen are hauling a catch of herring at an onshore fishing weir below, probably located at Weston's Point, which had a weir in 1895. Although fishing declined in the mid-19th century, seine nets, used predominantly after the Civil War, saw an increase in use.

Before shipbuilding at South Freeport, fishing was profitable. Alfred Soule and later Samuel Bliss packed 12,000 barrels per year of mackerel. As shipbuilding declined, Lewis & Bros. erected a steam-powered canning factory (at right above) at Dixon's Wharf in 1876, The company employed 95 people and paid about $2 per day for them to pack lobster, fish, clams, berries, and corn, according to the season, until about 1900. Dixon's Wharf, named for early 1900s owners, was previously named Waite's Wharf after Benjamin Waite, who came in 1797. Ironically, the wharf became a rum-running site during Prohibition while 10 Coast Guard rum-chasers were being built in the nearby Soule yard. Later, fisheries featured crabs as they became plentiful in lobster traps with changing environments. Bill and Alice Moody paid a penny per crab, hired women to pick, and sold crabmeat sandwiches at Kendall's Corner. From 1925 to 1932, Charles and John Hilton opened their own crabmeat factory at Porter's Landing (below).

Fred E. Ward (left above), from a family of shoemakers and farmers, worked in a variety of businesses. In 1892, he was a baker in the first of such ventures in town, the Freeport Bakery, owned by Will Lincoln and then by the Curtis brothers. The bakery was located in a small shop with an iron oven just north of Jameson Tavern. The building was moved next to the Warren Block around 1905, where it housed a barbershop and telephone office. Herman Gee is shown below delivering for the bakery around 1895. When the business failed, Ward worked as a shoemaker before becoming a clerk for Dillingham's Meat Market. A bakery was risky business judging by the number of people who tried it—from 1905 to 1910, Mary Bragdon, W.C. Anderson, O.G. Morse & Co., and the Moore brothers all had bakeries for a short time.

Tailor Fred Soule occupied the first floor of the Knights of Pythias building, shown above decorated for Freeport's 1889 centennial, until about 1915 when he moved to the Holbrook Block. A sign with the letters FCB once hung near the upper window, an acronym for the Pythian motto "Friendship, Charity, Benevolence." Harraseeket Grange No. 9 also held meetings here from 1901 until 1940, when members converted Kilby's cattle barn on Elm Street into a new hall. First chartered in 1874, the Grange initially met above two different stores on the Wardtown Road. Soule is shown below (third from left) posing with employees, from left, Mary Coffin, Fannie Dunham, and Nell Coffin. The others are unidentified. The firehouse on Mill Street was moved next to the Pythian hall around 1890, and there, it served as a hardware store and as I.S. Skillin's paper shoebox factory from 1912 to the 1930s. (Below, courtesy of Carolyn Ladd.)

By the late 19th century, drugstores had become an important commercial presence in Freeport. R.C. Farr, the first-known local apothecary, had a store in the Preble Oxnard (or Oxnard-Soule) Block from 1870 to 1873, followed by Briggs, Thomas, and Gore & Davis, who were druggists through the 1880s. In 1885, Winthrop Fogg began selling drugs and medicines in the Holbrook Block and stayed in business there until 1917. Shown above in front of his store during the 1889 celebration, Fogg is identified by an arrow. "Centennial ice cream" was available for 10¢, and a reading room drew patrons upstairs. The rare interior view below from around 1910, when the drugstore also served as the streetcar waiting room, shows, from left to right, Mr. Hanscom, Willis Merrill, and clerk Herbert Noyes. Fogg's partner Walter Cole took over the pharmacy and ran it as Rexall Drugs until 1943. After that, Johnson's Drugstore came in and stayed open until 1971.

William B. Coffin, a talented self-taught artist and avid baseball player, worked as a barber from 1896 to 1927. At the time he started hairdressing, Freeport already had six barbers, a sign that men were becoming interested in a groomed appearance. "Billy the Barber" is shown above in his Holbrook Block shop on March 17, 1900, cutting the hair of printer Frank Merrill, while Carleton Coffin waits. Billy later moved to the Warren Block, the one-story structure at right below with a striped barber pole, and worked there until his son Donald took over the business. Winfield Given owned the Warren Block, which housed a furniture store, undertaker, dentist, and the post office in 1901. Said to be the first glass-front post office in the United States, it was located directly beneath the L.L. Bean factory, which allowed mail to be delivered down a chute. (Above, courtesy of Donna J. Coffin.)

Above, from left to right, William Fish, Louis Curtis, and Verde Morton stand in the doorway of the Curtis & Fish grocery in the Nichols Block around 1895. Morton later joined as partner, and they moved to an adjacent store, where the fire started that burned the block in 1909. Fish became an undertaker and furniture store owner in the Warren Block around 1907, later moving to the new Davis Block. Curtis continued in the grocery business after the fire, running an IGA through 1943. In 1891, Charles Carr opened a drugstore in the Nichols Block, moved to the Mallet Block, and transferred to Thomas & Lunt around 1897. Harley Alden became the block's druggist from 1908 to 1918, followed by Roland Kimball, who was in business until it burned in 1946. Pictured below at Kimball's Drugstore around 1945 are, from left to right, Harold Walsh, Jack Gould, Kimball, Don Welch, and Myron Hilton.

H.E. Davis and Joseph Clark built the brick Davis and Clark Blocks following the 1909 fire that destroyed the wooden Nichols and Mallet Blocks. They agreed to start construction on the same day and managed to finish at the same time, forming Freeport's then-largest connected commercial structure. Clark had a heart attack before work began, but he signed papers from his sickbed. The bricks were made out-of-state and cost 11¢ each. After the block was completed, it housed L.L. Bean's shoe factory, a drugstore, tin shop, grocery, millinery, and restaurant, along with hardware, furniture, and clothing stores. Clark's Hotel hosted guests on the second and third floors. Despite its fire-resistant brick, the block burned twice more, in 1946 and 1981. Below is an interior view of Harley Alden's drugstore at the new block. Note its fine tin ceiling.

Above, store employees and proprietors pose in front of the newly built Oxnard Block in 1893, financed by John T. Oxnard, a gentleman and broker who inherited his sea captain father's wealth and home next door. The block, valued at $6,000 when it was new, housed four businesses on the ground floor and tenants upstairs. From left to right are H.W. Jones's jewelry store; George Preble's Fruit and Confectionery, which sold ice cream "with pure fruit flavors" for 5¢; a steam laundry; and Kendall & Stinchfield's meat market. Presbury Dennison and Charles T. Dillingham, shown with employees below, owned the Oxnard Block meat market from 1895 to 1896. In addition to meat, they sold flour, cigars, and tobacco. After pursuing other employment for a few years, Dillingham, whose father was a sea captain, owned and ran the meat market from 1899 to 1940.

Norman and Martha Nicholson moved to town in 1931 and made their living in the promising economic niches of industry, retail, and boarding. Norman was a shoe factory foreman and operated a confectionery and ice cream store in the Oxnard Block (pictured) until 1948. Martha opened their home on Main Street as a guesthouse, charging $1 per night. Nicholson's bed-and-breakfast is still in business today and is operated by granddaughter Jane and her husband, Alden Grant. (Courtesy of Jane Grant.)

Lunchrooms proliferated in Freeport following the shoe industry boom and rise of tourism in the early 20th century. Rose and Wallace Winslow (pictured) started Freeport Lunch on the north side of the Warren Block in 1917, and it was in business through 1928. The first known lunch service on Main Street was Pete's Lunchroom, opened in the Holbrook Block in 1898. Metcalfe's Lunch and the Corner Lunchroom followed soon after.

In 1885, Benjamin Conant moved to the c. 1780 Ammi Mitchell homestead, now part of the Harraseeket Inn on Main Street, where he raised Guernsey and Jersey dairy cows. Conant delivered milk and eggs to residents by wagon until his son Edgar, shown here, took over the business. Edgar is wearing Bean boots; he was the first person to test and approve the new product for L.L. Bean when he designed them in 1911.

Built by shipwright Samuel Wilson around 1852, this house on Route 1 near the Brunswick border became the site of Freeport's first gas station. Around 1910, Charles and Abbie Moseley installed two Socony pumps to service travelers between towns. Benjamin Pratt and his mother, Nora, had a store and restaurant here in the 1930s. Bob Hunter owned the first gas pump in Freeport Village, installed in front of the paper box factory around 1915.

Norman Kilby Jr. operated the Four Seasons Inn and Restaurant on Route 1 near Prout Road from about 1950 to 1960. He kept a monkey in the trees out back as a way to attract tourists and had a snappy sign that read, "The fish you eat here today slept last night in Casco Bay." The booming retail trade in Freeport Village kept numerous restaurants and motor courts in business, including several along this stretch, such as Roseland Cabins, across the road from Four Seasons, and Maine Idyll, a half mile toward Brunswick. Roseland Diner served fried clams, potatoes, tea, milk, coffee, and pie or ice cream for $1 in 1931. Roseland was in business from around 1930 to 1975, but Maine Idyll, which started in 1932, is still open and run by the same Marstaller family for more than 85 years.

This house at 123 Main Street was the homestead of Jonathan Cushing and was mostly built by him around 1799, a few years after he completed the Jameson Tavern. Orren W. Smith (right) bought it in 1887 and constructed a small two-story jewelry shop that he later rented as a bakery. Linwood Porter purchased the property in 1901, and the upstairs room of the shop served as a library until the new Bartol Library opened in 1906.

Blacksmith Samuel Andrews of Lisbon moved to Freeport in 1837, built a brick house on Main Street, and opened a shop and cider mill. He, with his sons Frank and John, was a village blacksmith from 1838 to the 1870s. He moved to Bow Street beside the tracks and built this shop on Middle Street around 1851. It was later used by blacksmith Herbert Noyes and served as Horace Nichols's garage before burning in 1974.

Four

COMMUNITY

The Rev. Alfred Johnson became the first ordained minister of Freeport's First Parish Church in 1789. He preached at the original meetinghouse, built in 1774 on Meetinghouse Road, until he moved to Belfast in 1805. During his tenure, Johnson raised $4,000 by subscription, which was more than the city of Portland, as part of an effort to locate Maine's first college in Freeport, a coup that was ultimately won by Brunswick.

Maine towns founded in the 18th century were under the Puritan government of Massachusetts, so their original churches were Congregational. Freeport's first meetinghouse, built in 1774, was used for ecclesiastical and town meetings. Located on a 100-acre lot set aside to support the Congregational ministry, it was accessed by the County Road that traversed the town in 1739 (Route 1) or by a road from Porter's Landing where people came by boat. Earlier residents journeyed as much as 10 miles to the Old Ledge Meetinghouse in Yarmouth. In 1818, a new church (pictured) was built in the center of the village on the current site of L.L. Bean. The nearby bandstand, well and pump, and stone enclosure that served as the town pound for roaming animals designate the area as community space. The church burned in 1894, and since Freeport Corner had become prime commercial property, it was rebuilt farther down Main Street. The original meetinghouse was dismantled, and the land, except the old parish burying ground, was sold to Daniel Cummings, a housewright who built the first Baptist church in 1808.

In the late 1700s, sectarian churches, particularly the Baptists, began to challenge the hegemony and doctrines of the Congregational Church. Baptist ministers preached in homes in Freeport, calling for adult baptism and questioning the need for college-educated ministers. A Baptist church was established in 1805, and a building erected in 1808 by housewright Daniel Cummings on land purchased from James Rogers. Before the church was completed, congregants met in Rogers's barn. The church grew, and a new structure was built on the site in 1897, which became a gathering place for groups such as the one above that included Eva Atwood, Clara Pratt, Laura Pratt, Mary Hilton, and Grace Pratt. Below, townspeople observe the ashes after the building burned in 1944. The current Baptist church was built in 1952, and the steeple added in 1965.

The Freewill Baptists organized in 1842 and dedicated a meetinghouse the following year on Wardtown Road next to the cemetery (pictured). Like the Methodists and Shakers, they believed that people chose their faith by free will, in contrast to the Congregationalists and Calvinist Baptists, who held that religious experience was predestined. No regular ministers were settled after about 1875, but the church continued through the early 20th century.

This Congregational Sunday school, enjoying a picnic above Pote's Wharf in 1902, includes Etta Pritham and Sumner Brewer, who are sharing the swing. Sumner was a schoolteacher and principal, and Etta was a cousin to brothers "Doc" Pritham and renowned chemist Charles Henry Pritham, who grew up at the Wolfe's Neck farmhouse. Alfred Pettengill (right of ladder) lived in the Pote House, where he was killed by lightning. (Courtesy of the Maine Historic Preservation Commission.)

This building on Upper Main Street has a long history of varied community uses. Constructed in 1811 as the first North Yarmouth Academy building, it was moved in 1847 to house a Methodist church and school. The building was transported to Freeport around 1867 and used by the Methodists until sold to the Universalists in 1884. Universalism was founded in 1805 by Mast Landing residents, the second of that denomination in Maine. The church met in five different locations and was periodically active until the 1970s, when its building was sold to become offices. Freeport schoolchildren are shown above using the church as temporary housing after the Maple Avenue school burned in 1916. Little is known about the King's Daughter Chapel (right) that once stood on Pleasant Hill Road. Dedicated in 1904, it fell into disuse and became dilapidated by the 1930s.

Annie May Collins, a photographer for F.E. Merrill, is shown above at the Bailey Schoolhouse on Wardtown Road where she attended as a child. Presumably, she staged this c. 1910 photograph as a memorial to the one-room schoolhouse after it closed in 1900. These schools had two doors, one for boys and one for girls. They were multiage classrooms, and the youngest children sat at the front. Many students only attended in the winter months when help with farm chores was not required. Bailey School students joined with the Gore School, on Old Brunswick Road near the intersection of Bragdon Road, to form the Bailey Gore School, shown below about 1901. From left to right are (first row) Clifford Morton, Roy Stevens, Ralph Cummings, Ernest Cannon, and Albert Bailey; (second row) Ruby Ward, Mildred Morton, and Winfield Given, (third row) Sam Sylvester, teacher Carrie Brackett, Bessie Bailey, and Laura Ward.

As people moved to the villages to work in the shoe-making and shipbuilding industries, village schools burgeoned, and outlying schools diminished. According to the 1898 town report, around the time the photograph above was taken, Pleasant Hill had the largest rural school and was still growing. Why this school countered the typical pattern is unknown. Pictured are, from left to right, (first row) Chester and John Ayer, Frank Lane, Guy Ringrose, Herbert Lane, Jeanette Allen, unidentified, George Kearney, unidentified, Inez Kincaid, and Edith Ayer, (second row) Harry and Frank Byram, Arthur Curtis, Thomas Ringrose, John Morrison, Harold Curit, Ada Morrison, Ina Curtis, Harriet Allen, and unidentified, (third row) unidentified, Henry Ringrose, Alphonso Merriman, George Ayer, Blanche Kincaid, Ethyl Lane, and teacher Mrs. Wade. Below is a rare early view of the interior of Grove Street School, built in 1894 to house the growing number of village students.

The original Mast Landing School was located on the north side of Flying Point Road as early as 1814. In 1861, a new school was built across the street on Ambrose Griffin's land. The c. 1895 photograph above shows, from left to right, (first row) Mildred Pettengill, Helen Cushing, Alice Curtis, Wieda Beele, Fredrica Byram, and Ellison Fletcher; (second row) Laura Cushing, Bertha Cushing, Florence Fletcher, Flossie Edwards, Maude Dyer, Carrie Townsend, Florence Griffin, and teacher Hattie Patterson. The original school was moved next to the bridge at the landing where it was used as a cooper's shop until the 1930s, when Albert Coffin hauled it back up the hill and remodeled it into a house. Below, on the opposite side of town, the Grover's Crossing or "neck" schoolchildren pose with teacher Mary Tuttle (center) around 1890.

The Old Ledge School (above) was built around 1832 on Pine Street in South Freeport. Widely believed to be the first and oldest schoolhouse, the town's other districts built schools at the same time when Freeport was incorporated in 1789. Children living in the area attended one school term per year starting in 1763, and before that, they traveled to the Old Ledge School in Yarmouth, built in 1736. South Freeport's Ledge School may be one of the earliest photographed, but others from the early 19th century may survive as houses, including one at Mast Landing. Schoolhouses were rebuilt as they aged or were outgrown, and the "first period" buildings were repurposed as shops or outbuildings. The Central School (below) on the Old County Road was remodeled into a house, as were the Porter's Landing, Collins, Pleasant Hill, and Grover's Crossing Schools.

When the original schoolhouse was outgrown, another high school was built in 1918 at the end of Howard Place (above) at a cost of $25,000. The American Legion and Lenox Shoe used the first building until it burned in 1930. Emma Dawson was appointed principal at the new school, the first female to hold that position, a sign of women's rights emerging at the time. Baccalaureate and graduation exercises were held at the Baptist and Congregational churches, respectively. Initially, eighth-grade students shared the building, and later, grades six through eight comprised North Grammar School. The students performed an annual operetta, including *Robin Hood* in 1941 (below) and *The Jolly Tars* the following year. An addition to the school was built in 1941, and the building became the junior high when a third high school was constructed in 1962.

Freeport High School's first girls' basketball team was organized in 1912, inspired by the boys' first team in 1910. The girls lost every game, but the team turned around under Coach Flewelling. In 1914–1915, they captured glory for the school by winning 9 of 11 games. Players Varney, Fogg, Chase, Loring, Brown, Groves, Fish, Lavers, Tracy, Bibber, and Winslow were considered the best girls' team to represent the school.

Young men who served during World War I were often high school athletes. They were locally revered and sometimes returned from service to coach high school teams, as shown in this photograph of the 1917–1918 Freeport High basketball team. From left to right are Mahlon Walsh, Everett Curtis, Fred Snow (holding ball), Ted Curtis, Stanwood Fish, and Coach Allen Mansfield, a World War I lieutenant and Freeport High graduate.

Baseball, the first athletic activity at Freeport High School, was organized in the late 1880s when the sport was popular throughout the country. In this pre-1901 photograph, the team plays in a field in front of the original high school, which faced Park Street. In 1893, a tennis team was organized, as was a football team, although the latter made little progress until the following year. Football Eleven, so called since 11 players were needed, included players Pritham and Tyler (ends), Mallett and Banks (tackles), Williams and Dennison (guards), Soule (center), Small (quarterback), T. Randall (fullback), and J. Randall, Davis, and Means (halfbacks) shown below posed on the steps of town hall in 1896. According to the school yearbook the *Clarion*, the team did not always win but "made a very creditable showing," taking three of nine games and tying one.

The Women's Movement inspired Freeport High School to start a domestic club that taught skills in preparation for a vocation in cookery, millinery, or dressmaking, and for practical housekeeping. This c. 1930 group included, from left to right, (first row) Emma Wilson, Alice Dyer, Doris Jackson, and teacher Mildred Bubar; (second row) Mildred Knight, Irene Henshaw, Harriet Brewer, and Ada Conant; (third row) Harriet Bennett and teacher Theda Ray.

George and Mildred Soule gave land for the new Soule School in South Freeport after the grammar school was razed in 1956. In this 1957 photograph, Mrs. Hopkins's class is having a formal tea party. Peter Corcoran, principal from 1976 to 1979, brought an innovative multiage program that focused on environmental education and the total community as a learning classroom. In 1991, the school moved to a new building at Mast Landing.

The Freeport Lodge of Masons was chartered in 1816 and included Joseph Porter, who transferred his membership from Liverpool. Like Porter, many of the original members were master mariners, perhaps because of their contacts in England where masonry was founded. The Masons first met in the ell of Solomon Dennison's house at Mast Landing, and later above the Bailey store and Gore & Holbrook store on Main Street, until the latter burned around 1844, destroying the organization's records. After decades meeting at different locations, the Masons built a new hall on Mechanic Street in 1874, now Brown Goldsmiths. Mason Charles Dillingham is shown at left at the hall preparing a bean supper in 1935. The Knights of Pythias had an auxiliary women's group known as the Pythian Sisters. Posing at their lodge in the 1940s (below), the women don Pythian temple jewels indicating longevity with the organization.

Until the 1930s New Deal reforms, individual towns provided for their poor. By 1857, Freeport supported a poor farm for indigent people on Hunter Road; it was overseen by a superintendent. The farm burned in 1878 and was moved to the True-Titcomb house off Route 136 in 1885 (pictured). Peter Stevens was the first overseer, and George Richards was the last. In 1903, the farm housed 112 "tramps" in an old hen house.

Elizabeth "Dib" Hyde, daughter of Dr. Nathan Hyde, organized and led the Harraseeket Campfire Girls from 1913 to 1918. The "maidens" had Indian names and outfits and met around a campfire. They performed plays, discussed historical figures, and kept a scrapbook of outings to the quarry, shipyard, and Casco Castle. Pictured are Agnes Dunning, Alice True, Pearl Libby, Julia Bailey, Helen Strout, Mildred Coffin, Delia Bowden, Alveda Groves, and Helen Dillingham with leader "Dib" Hyde in the back row at right.

During World War II, male and female civilians manned airplane observation posts to watch for enemy aircraft 24 hours a day. This post was built on Wardtown Road in 1942, and a similar station was located on the Old County Road. A third post atop the water tower on Cushing Avenue was accessed by an external stairway. Volunteers were trained to identify specific planes and to call by radio when any were seen.

The Frost Gully pumping station was built in 1892 as Freeport's first public water supply. Since Freeport Village had grown into a busy commercial district with shoe factories and many other businesses, entrepreneur E.B. Mallet helped finance and develop a municipal water system as a measure against fire. The system had four miles of water mains, 18 hydrants, a storage tank on Maple Avenue, and this steam-powered pumping station.

Freeport's firefighters are posed above in front of the fire station on Cushing Avenue with their firetruck and trophies won at a muster in 1932. The station building (below) was moved to the site by oxen from the Cushing Briggs shipyard in 1899. It was built around 1860 and had served as a sail loft. The hose tower for drying hoses was added onto the station at its new location. Moved near the train depot in 1995, the tower now functions as an information center for Freeport visitors. The bell at the top of the tower was used as the town's fire alarm system until the mid-1950s. Isaac Skillin, who owned the adjacent home, liked to shoot at the bell with a pistol to make it ring. Ike's friend MacMillan gave his daughter Hester the young blue fox she holds below about 1925.

Marching bands became a popular expression of patriotism in the decades following the Civil War. Around 1879, veteran Henry Miller organized the Harraseeket Band, originally the Freeport Coronet Band, with Davis brothers Henry (leader), Frank, Ansel, and Will; Cushing brothers Harris, Dana, and Henry; Soule brothers Ed, E.S., George A., and George E.; and friends John Kendall, Charles Chase, Benjamin Chandler, Jerry Talbot, Elroy Libby, and Harlan Dennison. Samuel Cushing, the Davis brothers' shoe-making business partner, started his own band the following year. The Harraseeket Band played for the annual Merchants' Day picnic, Memorial Day, and the town's centennial celebration on July 4, 1889, after which it disbanded until 1906. Their uniforms were blue frock coats, gold-striped trousers, and capes with white plumes. Charles, Jeremiah, and Ed Chase, a Porter's Landing contingent of the band, are shown below in 1908 proudly donning GAR and Grange regalia.

Freeport's first municipal hall was located over the Gore & Holbrook store, built around 1831 at Main and Mechanic Streets. Before that, town meetings were held at the Congregational church. The store burned around 1844, and a new town hall was built on Park Street in 1848 for about $1,200. Six men bid on the construction, but it is unknown who was chosen. Ship joiner Ambrose Curtis was the probable builder as he traveled to California seeking gold just after construction. The interior of the hall (above) shows the Civil War monument ready to be placed outside. The dedication ceremony on May 26, 1906, featured Joshua Chamberlain delivering the address, while the Harraseeket Band entertained the crowd (below). The Grand Army of the Republic, organized in 1885, met twice a month at the town hall shown in the distance. The building also served as the school's gymnasium from 1920 to 1941.

Parades have been popular community events in Freeport since the 19th century. The parade above featured exotic animals—an elephant, camels, and even a tapir painted on the side of a wagon. Signs indicate the year was between 1911 and 1914, but it is unknown what occasion this unusual parade is celebrating. If the year is 1914, it may be marking Freeport's 125th anniversary. The parade shown below is part of the town's statehood centennial celebration. Freeport was one of 69 towns statewide that organized major events for Maine's 100th anniversary in 1920. L.L. Bean's brother Guy was in charge of decorations and publicity, and E.B. Mallet was the planning chairman. The activities scheduled for June 21–26 included ball games, a free clambake, "pictures" and dancing at the Nordica Theater, and a lecture at the Baptist church by renowned Arctic explorer Donald MacMillan, a graduate of Freeport High School.

Five

PASTIMES AND TRAVELING

Casco Castle, built in 1903 for $20,000, encouraged tourists to ride the trolley, which was established the previous year. Overlooking the Harraseeket River in South Freeport, the resort accommodated 100 guests at about $3 per day and boasted gardens, swimming, boating, telephones, orchestral music, a restaurant, baseball field, zoo (with bison, monkeys, and wolves), and access by trolley and steamboat. This 1908 photograph shows attendees at a campaign rally for Bert Fernald, candidate for governor.

When the electric railway was planned to connect Brunswick and Yarmouth, the line was built through South Freeport, a less direct route, in hopes of facilitating transportation between the villages. Shown on South Freeport Road (above) with the Congregational church at right, the trolley offered students a 10-minute ride to the high school and improved travel to and from the railroad depot. Developer Amos Gerald also meant the streetcars to bring tourists to a resort he planned the year after the line was established in 1902. Shown below, the Casco Castle was accessed from a trolley stop in a nearby field that included a waiting room with awning and a dramatic entrance over moat-like Spar Creek, via a 306-foot-long suspension bridge. The footbridge once spanned the Androscoggin River between Lewiston-Auburn before Gerald purchased it for use at the castle.

The electric railway came to Freeport in 1902 and ran from Brunswick to Yarmouth via Freeport Village and South Freeport until 1929. This 1906–1909 photograph shows summer trolley riders disembarking at Freeport Square on the day of the annual Merchants' Day picnic, an event that drew hundreds of people. The scene is reminiscent of the crowds of visitors during the summer months of present-day Freeport.

The steamer *Maquoit*, much loved by summer people, was built in South Portland in 1904. It provided service between Portland, South Freeport, Harpswell Center, and Mere Point, as well as to the islands of Chebeague, Little John, Birch, and Bustins. This view shows the steamship coming into the dock at the town wharf in South Freeport about 1910. Wolfe's Neck is in the distance.

The electric carbarn was built on Lower Main Street in 1902 to power and house the trolleys. Originally the Portland & Brunswick Street Railway, the line was sold to the Lewiston, Augusta & Waterville Railway in 1913, which retained ownership until 1919. Growing popularity of the automobile meant the streetcars struggled for business, but the line was kept going by the Androscoggin & Kennebec Railway for another decade. When the trolleys were discontinued in 1929, this building fittingly became the carbarn garage. Freeport's town office was located here until it moved to the old Grove School in 1988 and this building was replaced by a new structure for the fire station. The carbarn also housed a trolley plow, shown below removing snow from the tracks at Freeport Square in the early 1900s.

The trolleys ran year-round in Freeport, using heated cars in winter and open cars in summer. In 1902, there were four and seven of each type, reflecting heavier use in the summertime. Locals often rode the streetcars during winter storms since they ran when roads were impassable. Ronald Cummings's father, Henry, was a motorman, and Ron recalled loving to ride the trolleys in the winter because of the way the cars followed tracks hidden by snow and magically curved to the side when it seemed they would go straight. Shown above on Lower Main Street with Mallet's house in the distance, this winter car is speeding toward its next stop in Freeport Village. The winter crew is shown below in front of the waiting room beneath Harraseeket House in 1903 with superintendent Rice (left) and William Anderson, a painter, next to him wearing a heavy fur coat.

In 1827, John Tuttle purchased 130 acres of land and built this farm, where he raised potatoes and sheep. The homestead was passed to his son James in 1853 and, later, to James's son-in-law Andrew Rogers, a cooper who also raised meat, shown above with his family in 1882. Thin topsoil and erosion caused by overgrazing led to exposure of the underlying glacial silt. The depleted farmland was sold to Henry Goldrup in 1925, and he developed the dunes into a tourist attraction, the Desert of Maine. The barn is the only structure remaining today. With the popularity of automobile travel in the 20th century, the desert became a favorite destination, and Charles Coffin exploited the opportunity by billing himself as the "Maine hermit." He charged tourists to visit his nearby house, pictured below, where he played a homemade piano-organ and sold curios.

The Harraseeket River has long been a source of imagination for adults and children alike since its first role as provider of transportation, fish, mill power, and shipbuilding sites. Later, inhabitants expanded use of the river beyond their economic needs to include recreational activities, like boating, fishing, and swimming. These children are playing with homemade boats in South Freeport.

Freeport's World Beaters baseball team captured the championship in 1908. The players were, from left to right, (seated) Reuel Hanscome, Glendon Small, Edwin Small, and Arthur Griffin; (standing) Willis Snow, Nathan Kendall, Clyde Mitchell, Charles Luce, Linwood Porter, and Charles "Judge" Keen. According to a 1931 newspaper, they were "not too well liked by the other baseball clubs of Maine and New England," presumably because they were a first-rate team that often won.

Ira Coffin of Porter's Landing owned a photography studio at the corner of Middle and School Streets from 1878 to 1899. His son George Coffin and Charles Harris followed in the business after that. Ira took these studio photographs of a theatrical group and a man with a bicycle in the 1890s, recording two popular forms of entertainment at the time. The Jolly Seven (above) was made up of young performers from Porter's Landing and included, from left to right, (seated) Margaret Soule, Della Chase, and Mertie Ring; (standing) Fred Dillingham, Ernest Soule, Charles Brown, Albra Chase, Willis Coffin, and Herbert Dillingham. Photographs of people posing with bicycles were common in the late 19th century, a reflection of the enthusiasm for this new kind of transportation. By 1895, two village stores sold bicycles, and an 1890s touring book shows a six-mile route from Freeport to Yarmouth along a "clay" road.

Minnow "Minnie" Brook Hall was a community building at Porter's Landing where residents gathered for bean suppers, dances, and entertainments of various kinds. The musical, theatrical, and comedic events were so popular that people attended from other neighborhoods. The hall was born from a building formerly used for learning and art, the Old Ledge Schoolhouse, previously located on Pine Street in South Freeport. The building had also once housed the workshop of ship carver Emery Jones. Horses hauled the building to its new location on South Street, just east of Minnow Brook. Community members, shown above in front of the hall around 1908, contributed money and time, starting with installation of a kitchen. Pictured below, from left to right, Charles, Ed, Quincy, and Jerry Chase are dressed as cooks for a performance. Expenses eventually became too high, and the hall was sold in 1925 and razed in 1940.

Actor Frederick E. Mortimer and his wife, Jennie, theater enthusiasts from Biddeford, opened the Photoplay Theater about 1911. It featured moving pictures, illustrated songs, and vaudeville acts. Originally located on the Davis Block roof, it was renamed the Nordica in 1916 after the Maine-born opera singer Lillian Nordica. Around 1920, the theater moved to a new Bow Street building that later had a disruptive connected bowling alley (left). It was in business until 1968 and the structure burned five years later. In 2011, a new Nordica theater opened on Depot Street, and the first film shown was *Twilight*. The Photoplay ball team (below) was sponsored by the original theater. Pictured around 1912 are players, from left to right, (first row) Whitney, Millet, Walsh (captain), Whitney, and Snow; (second row) Johnson, Curtis, Wetmore, and Liscord. Mahlon "Babe" Walsh played baseball recreationally for years and became a local barber. (Above, courtesy of Lincoln Merrill Jr.)

This photograph shows "three little maids" from the opera *Mikado* performed in Freeport in 1892. At least seven local amateur actors and actresses starred in the production, including, from left to right, Bertha Dillingham Pinkham (whose husband Ernest played "Poobah"), Stella Soule, and Anna Stockbridge. Bertha's father, John Dillingham, was a sea captain, and her brother Monroe died in Andersonville prison during the Civil War.

From left to right, Larry Randall and brothers Ned, Paul, and Albert "Brud" Coffin pose atop a fishing boat moored near the Lufkin-Kelsey house at Mast Landing. Here, the boat is serving as their diving platform for a river swim. Ned and his brothers became local builders, and he served in the Senate. Known as the "Eel Skinner," a self-imposed pen name, Ned wrote humorous and historical articles for the *Shopping Notes*.

The Freeport Park Association organized its first agricultural fair and exhibition in 1895. The fairgrounds were located on Pleasant Street and included a racetrack that became a natural skating rink when the park fell into disuse around 1917. Harry Merrill, who ran Mitchell's livery and served as the organization's president for years, is shown at the track around 1900 with his racehorse and bicycle-wheeled buggy, a popular racing vehicle at the time.

The 1889 centennial featured an old-timers' baseball game comprised of players 50 and older. Enthusiasm for the sport led to the organization of a town baseball team soon after. This c. 1895 team included several high school players who had graduated. Baseball in the 19th century followed different rules, including the twist that an out was counted whenever a running player was touched with the ball, which was usually thrown at him.

Lobster and clambakes on the Harraseeket River have been a popular summertime activity for generations. The Skillin family and friends are shown above with lobsters and a roasting fire pit between the rocks on June 8, 1919, near Alfred Perry Taylor's cottage on the ocean side of Wolfe's Neck. Young Eddie Skillin is at center. Below, Gertrude (left) and Bertha Skillin are digging for clams on the river side of the peninsula, at a location just off the point known as the cove at Pumpkin Knob. (Both, courtesy of John W. Skillin.)

This group of ladies and a few children are enjoying an outing at Wolfe's Neck on the porch of the H.E. Davis cottage around 1915. Their version of summertime fun included a game called "how to eat donuts the hard way," which involved a race to eat donuts hanging from a string.

The Harraseeket River has provided a means of transportation by canoe or boat for centuries. Before good roads were available, people traveled by water. In 1739, town officials traveling in a canoe identified more than a dozen squatters. Recreational boating became popular when tourism boomed in the late 1800s. This family, wearing outfits for swimming or "bathing" as it was then called, vacationed in a cottage on Bartol Island around 1900. (Courtesy of David Coffin.)

The earliest settlers to the area inhabited the islands of Casco Bay, where they fished and traveled by water before inland areas were cleared. Bustins Island was named for John Bustin, who lived there around 1660 until he sold to William Haines of Flying Point. James and Johanna Bibber of Harpswell bought the island in 1797 and built the first surviving farmhouse, shown at left around 1895. They used oxen to clear the land and farmed and fished for over 50 years. Starting in 1888, the steamer *Phantom* began servicing the island, and it quickly became an established summer colony with a store and restaurant. The first summerhouse was built in 1892, and many others followed including the Pidge Cottage, which had a popular swimming cove (below). Donald MacMillan started a nautical boy's camp in 1903 that was attended by future Broadway legend Cole Porter.

The flat-bottomed boat transporting men, women, a child, horse, cow, and wagon was typical of the type commonly used on the Harraseeket River in the 18th and 19th centuries. The gundalow served as a truck for hauling livestock, cordwood, hay, fish, and bricks by water. Square ends and propulsion by rowing were features unique to this area, differing from the lateen-rigged double-ended gundalows used on the Kennebec and Piscataqua Rivers.

The King's Highway, a horse path through the woods in the 1680s, was Freeport's first thruway. A similarly crude County Road was laid in 1739, and today's Route 1 largely follows its path. Even after improvements, future president John Adams was painfully "incumbered" when he traveled the road in 1765. This crew experienced some of his frustration on the same route 150 years later (near the Freeport-Brunswick line) when their work wagon got stuck.

Winter weather can make roads difficult to pass in Maine. This photograph following a springtime storm shows an extreme example of a snow-laden road in North Freeport on April 19, 1922. Confirming the centuries-old adage, "Neither snow nor rain nor heat nor gloom of night stays these couriers from the swift completion of their appointed rounds," Rural Free Delivery carrier Jesse Ward is pictured delivering mail by wagon.

The oldest existing road in Freeport, Route 1, has been well-traveled for nearly three centuries. Especially busy before the interstate came through in 1957, regular road work has been required over time. In the 1930s, the Lane Construction Company improved the historic road by building an under-layer of cement using a system of steel grids as forms. Workers are shown here pouring a cement slab near Frost Gully in 1931.

When parcel post delivery began in 1913, L.L. Bean realized the opportunity and started a mail-order business, shipping Freeport's first package. In 1920, the company made up 37 percent of Freeport's mail, and by 1934, it reached 74 percent. One day's shipment is shown at the depot in 1950; soon after, the company acquired to its own baggage car. Freight service has been uninterrupted since 1849, largely because of Bean's mail order business.

Organized in 1836, the Portland & Kennebec Railroad planned a line from Portland to Augusta through Freeport. Passenger and freight service began in 1849 and had a profound effect on the town's economic development, paving the way for the village to prosper as a pipeline of trade. This engine is shown in front of Mallet's shoe factory, which imported shoe parts and exported shoes by rail starting in 1886.

This rare view above of the town's first railroad depot shows the telegraph and, later, telephone office, (1892 and 1895, respectively), the two-story structure at left. A one-story passenger station, built in 1849, was located behind it. Side tracks carried freight cars to the loading area of the gristmill just beyond and to the freight house between. At that time, bricks, milk, hay, apples, granite, lumber, shoes, shingles, and Christmas trees were exported from Freeport by rail, and potatoes, cement, and vast quantities of coal were imported to power the steam engines used in manufacturing. This station burned in 1910, and a new depot (below) was built the following year. In 1961, it was moved to Boothbay to serve as a railroad museum following the demise of passenger service in 1959. Amtrak's *Downeaster* brought a new station and service in 2012.

With the increased traffic along Route 1 due to tourism and a busy shoe industry in Freeport Village, the railroad crossing in Freeport became particularly dangerous. This photograph shows the Maine Department of Transportation constructing an overpass on Upper Main Street near Summer Street in 1937.

Shown around 1900 are Freeport employees of the Maine Central Railroad, including James W. Coffin with a soot-blackened face in the back row and Daniel Rodick to his right. Coffin was a fireman who shoveled coal into the engine to keep it running. He also worked as a coal man unloading the coal pockets near the depot. From about 1906 to 1950, he was an engineer, conducting the train from Bangor to Union Station.

Freeport section crew members, from left to right, Arthur Holbrook, Leonard Holbrook, unidentified, Percy Holbrook, George Eastman, and Foreman James Doucette pose with their pump car in front of a toolhouse on the Maine Central Railroad line about 1900. The Holbrook brothers, three of eight sons (and one daughter) born to William Augustus and Lydia Holbrook, also worked as lobstermen, in the shoe factories, and making tools for Bath Ironworks.

This unusual view of engine and coal car stopped on Bow Street shows the engineer looking up the road toward Main Street. The photograph was taken after 1893 since the Oxnard Block is visible in the distance. Two young children have passed under the gate and appear to be planning to cross just in front of the train, an indication of different cultural attitudes about independence and safety a century ago.